Foreword

KENT is rightly famous for its reputation as the Garden of England and its beauty has long been an inspiration for artists and writers.

The county's landscapes and seascapes are irresistible for those modern-day artists the photographers, who have inundated Kent on Sunday with pictures since we started to run our Images of Kent feature.

Indeed, such was the popularity of the weekly photographic feature in the newspaper, it was not long before we were planning an exhibition of some the best photographs at one of Kent's most stunning locations, Leeds Castle.

The popular photographic show was a chance for photographers to show off their hard work, and for the public to enjoy some wonderful shots of their county.

Thanks are due to Leeds Castle, Canon which sponsored the event and provided photographic prizes for the competition that ran with the show, and to Kingsferry Picture Framers which mounted the photographs for the show.

This book is intended to celebrate the scenery of Kent and the talent and enthusiasm of all the photographers who made it possible.

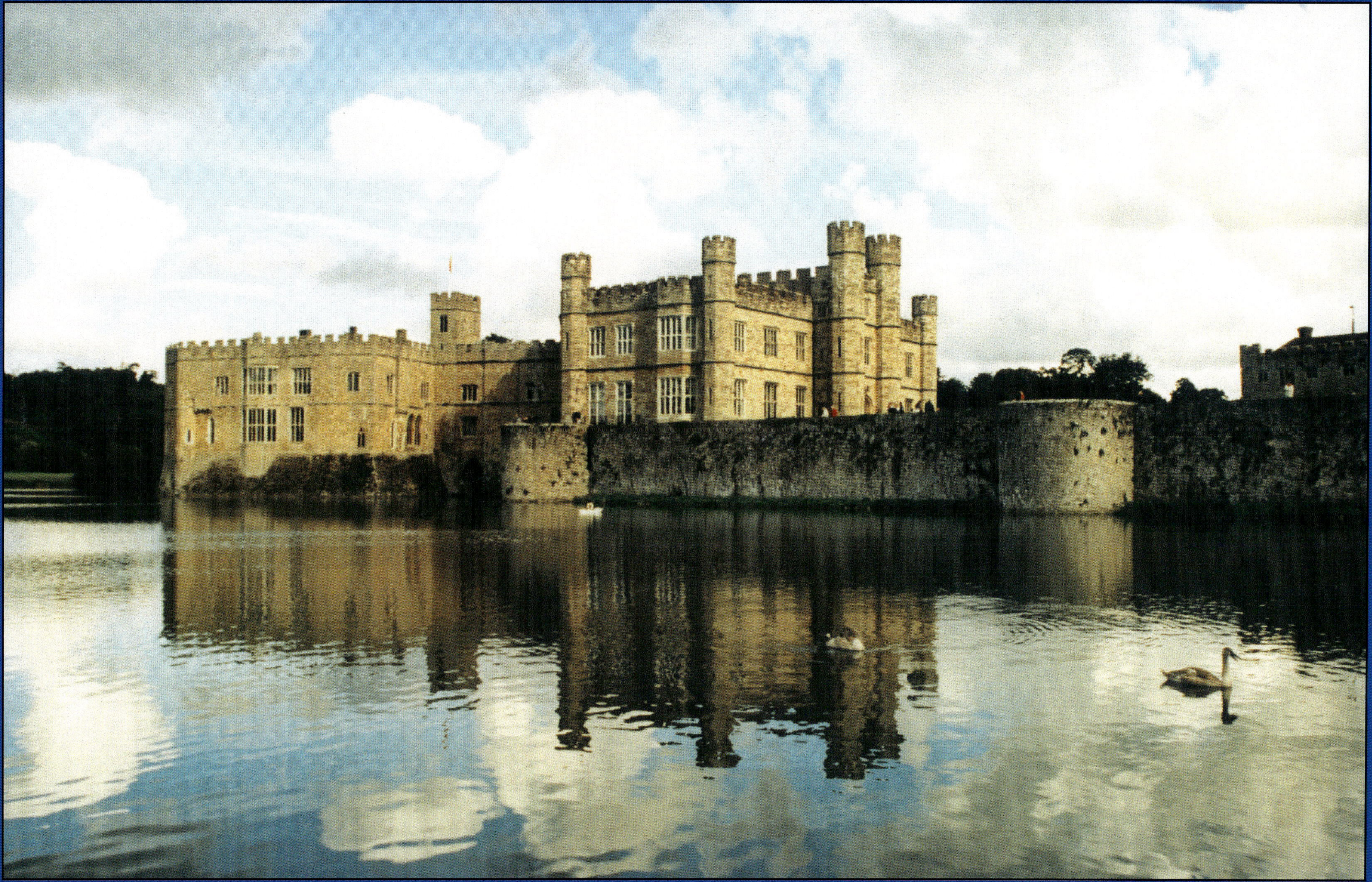

5 Leeds Castle, Maidstone

Photo by OT Mannion

images of Kent

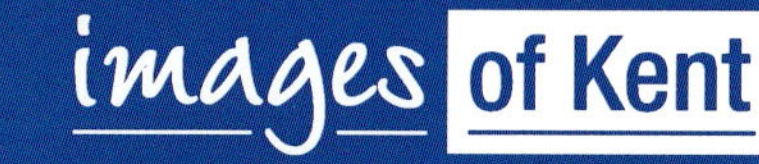

Photo by David Bowie

Photo by Larry Bains

images of Kent

Photo by Pam Penfold

images of Kent

Photo by Den Johnson

Photo by Phil Houghton

images **of Kent**

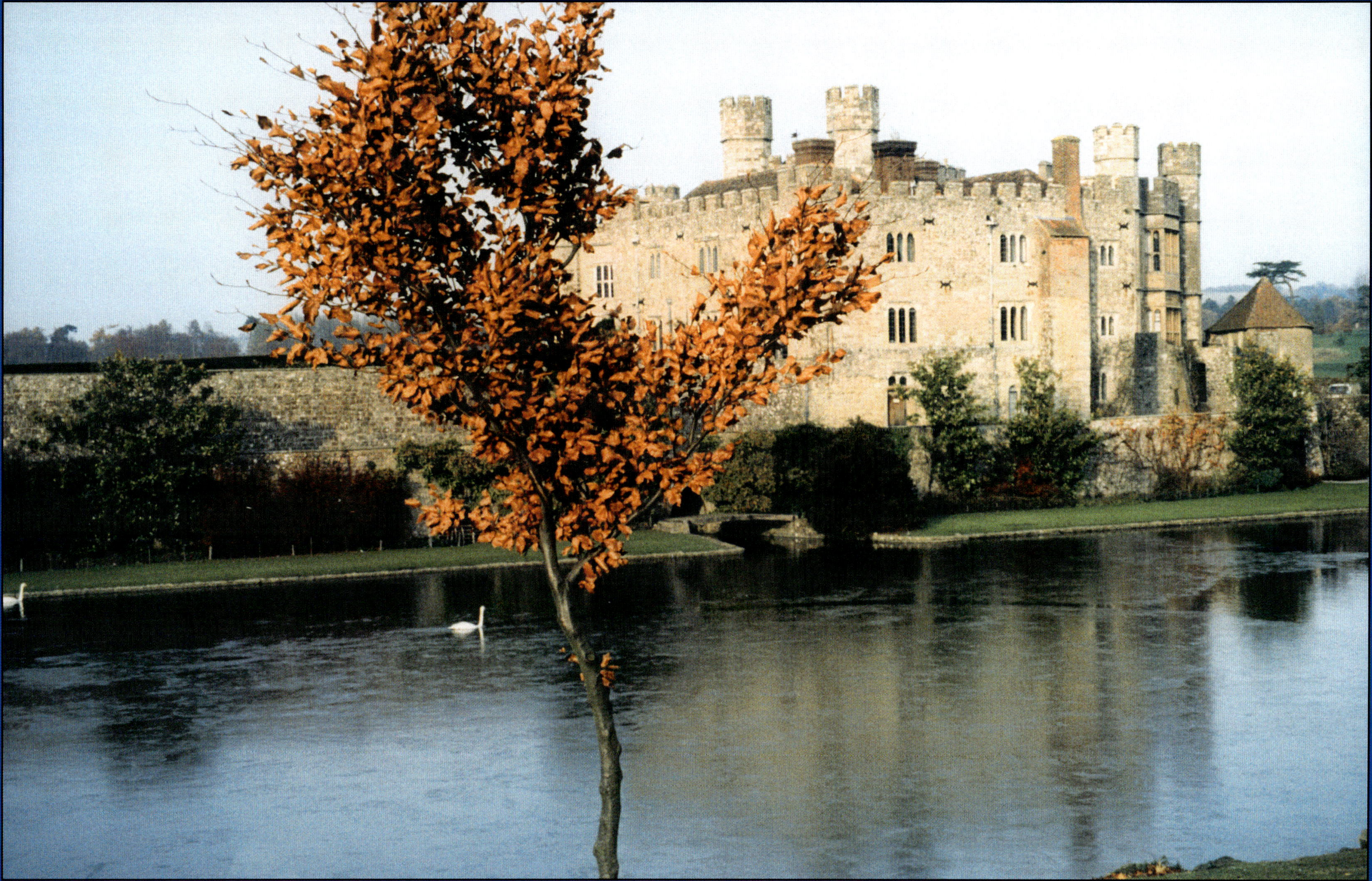

 Leeds Castle, Maidstone

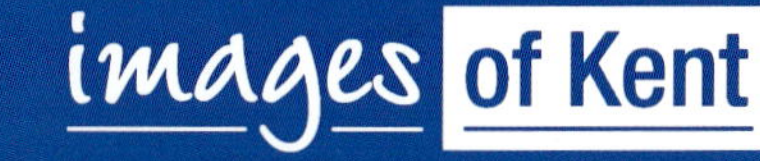

Photo by H Wouldham

 Frosty morning at Broomfield pond

Photo by David Crippen

 Kearsney

photo by Phil Houghton

images **of Kent**

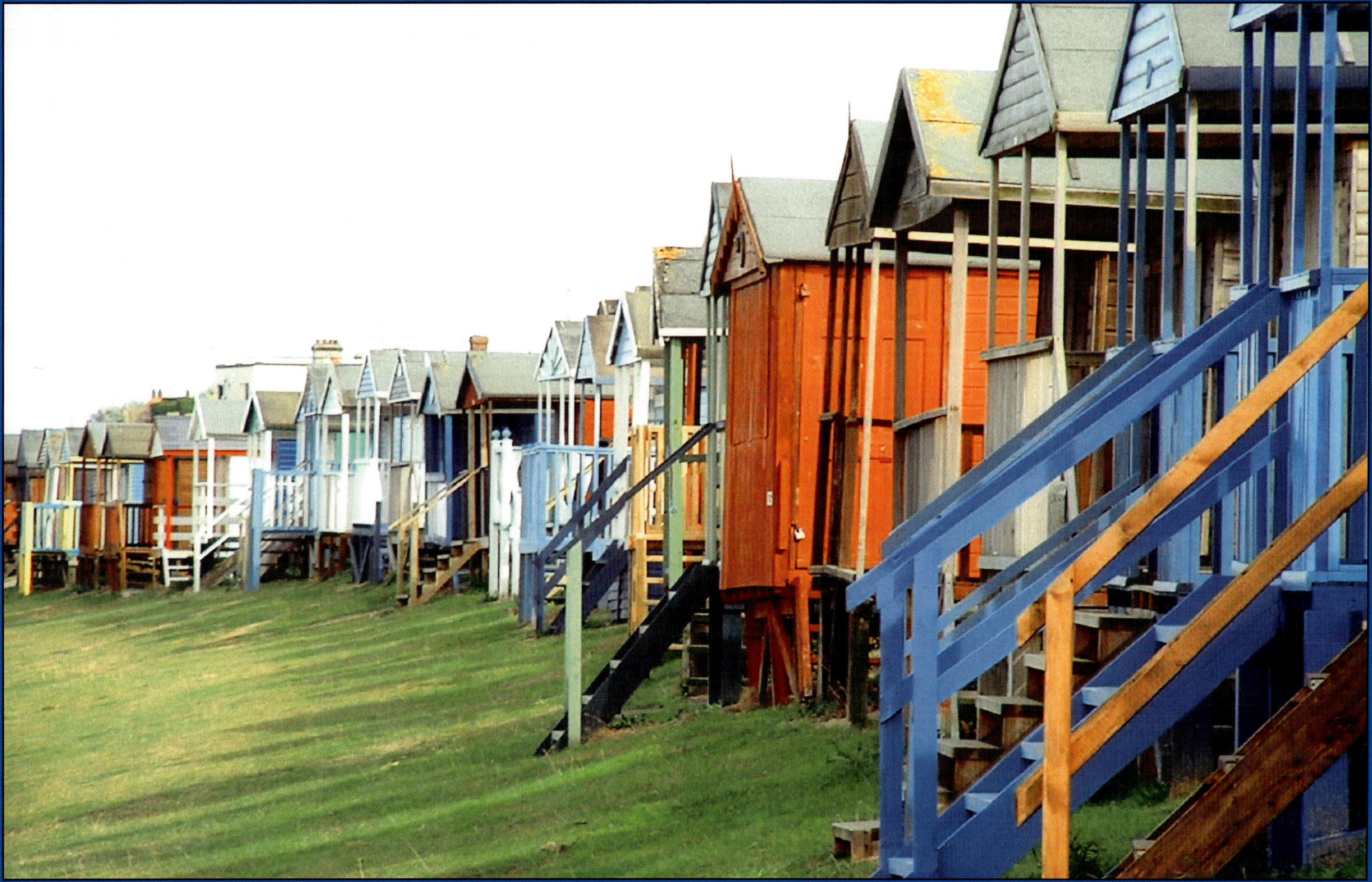

Photo by Geoffrey Dean

images **of Kent**

Photo by Colin Miles

images of Kent

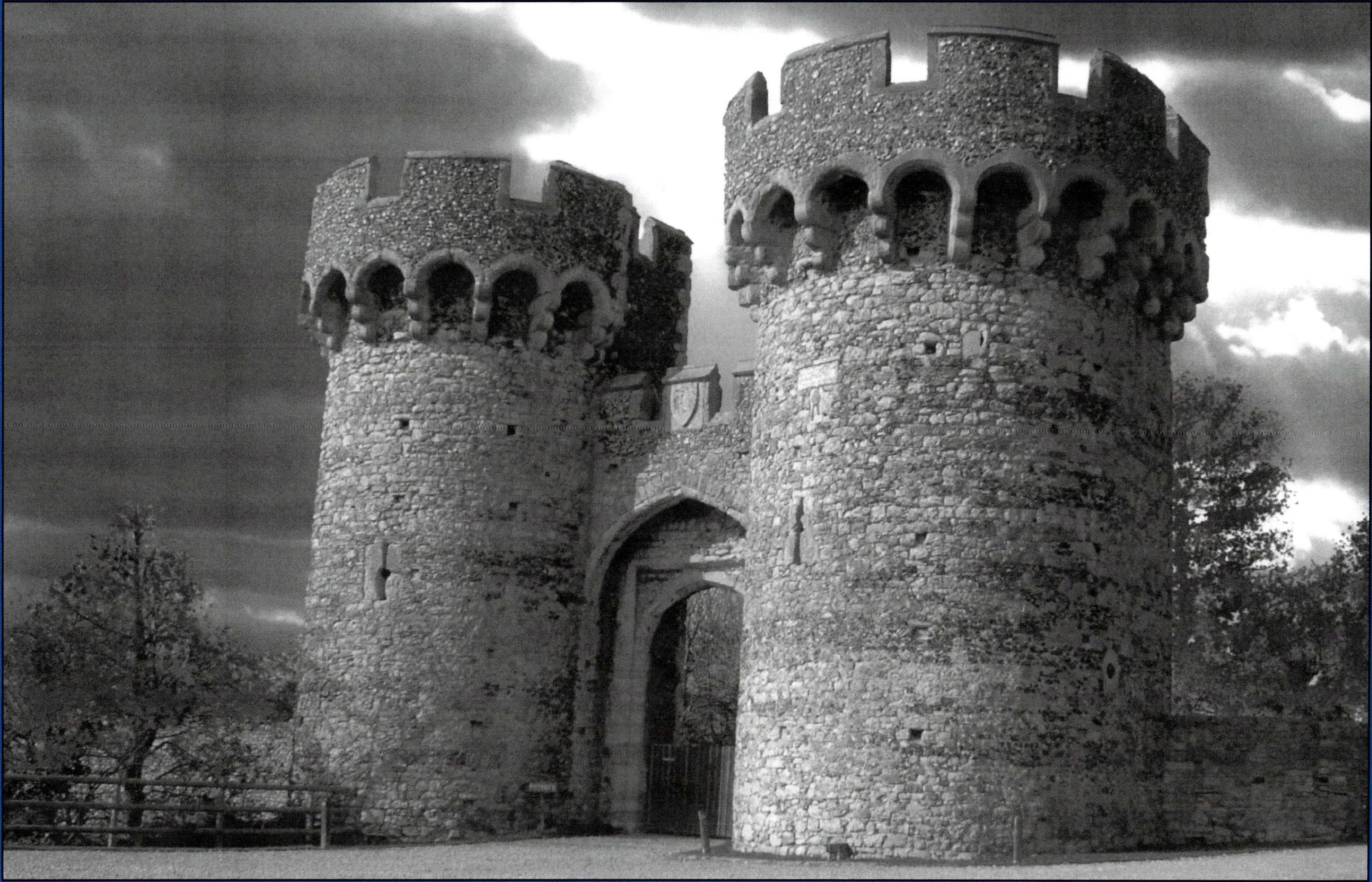

Photo by Andrew Whittaker

images of Kent

Photo by Damon Nielsen

    Richborough   Photo by Phil Houghton   *images* of Kent

Photo by Christopher Allison

images of Kent

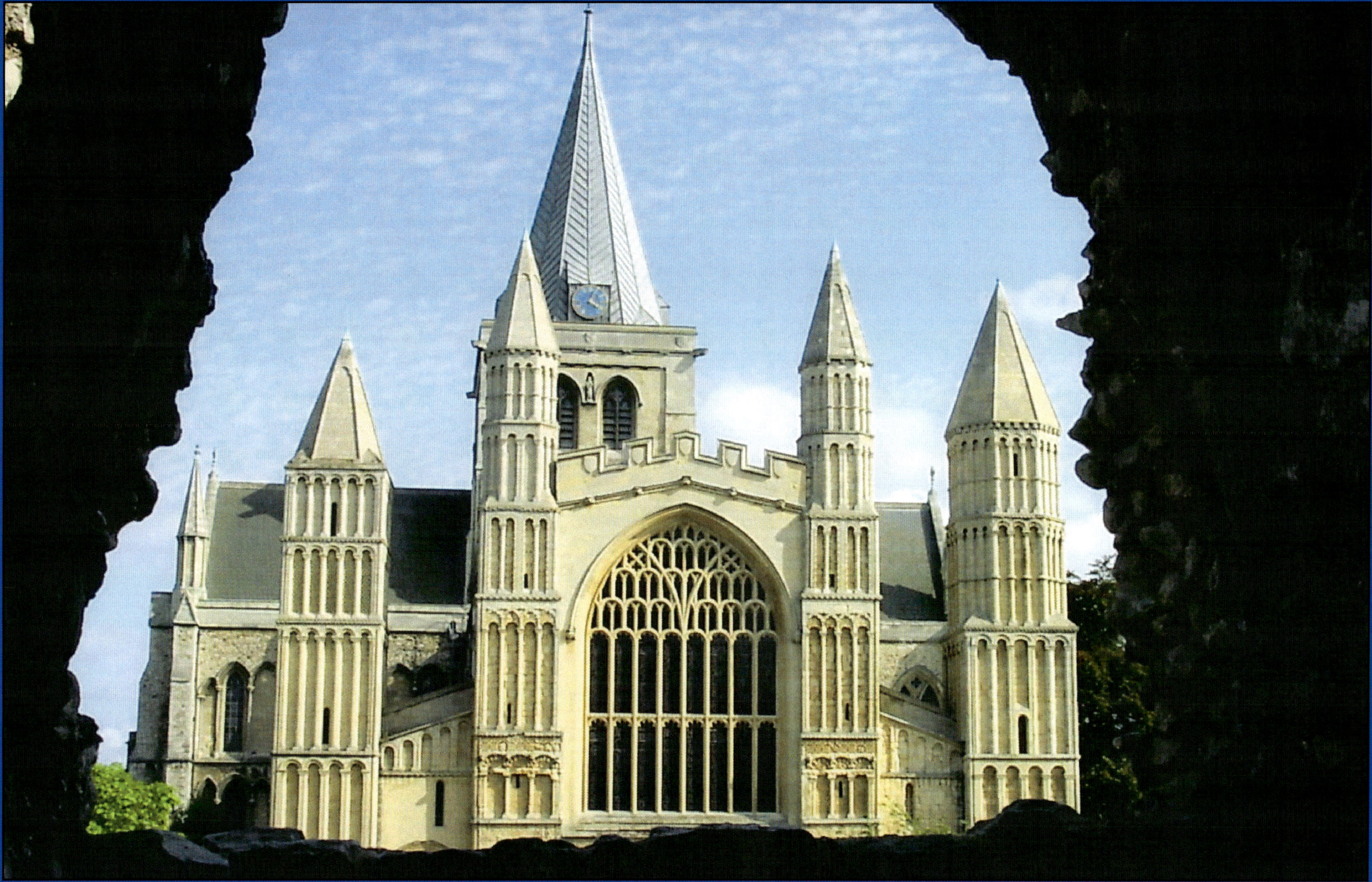

Photo by Lynn Hill

images **of Kent**

    Butterfly

Photo by Phil Houghton

Photo by Keith Thompson

images **of Kent**

Photo by Neil Rutherfoord

images of Kent

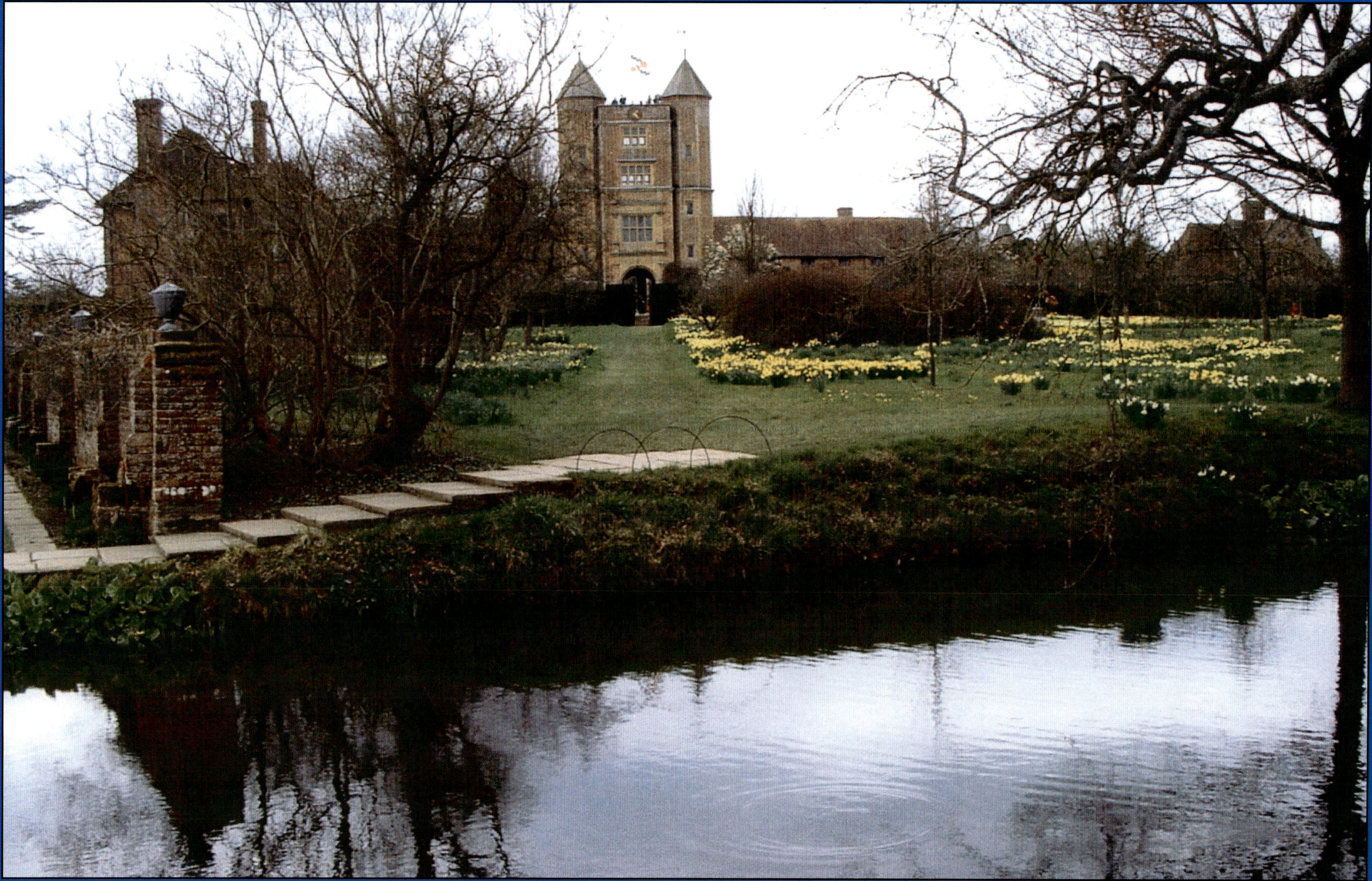

43 Sissinghurst Castle

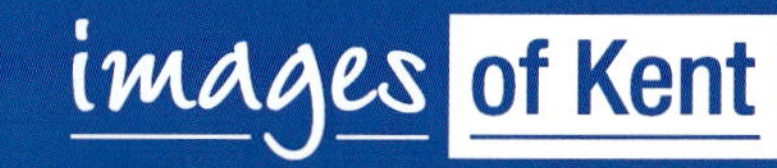

Photo by D Godden

Photo by David Bowie

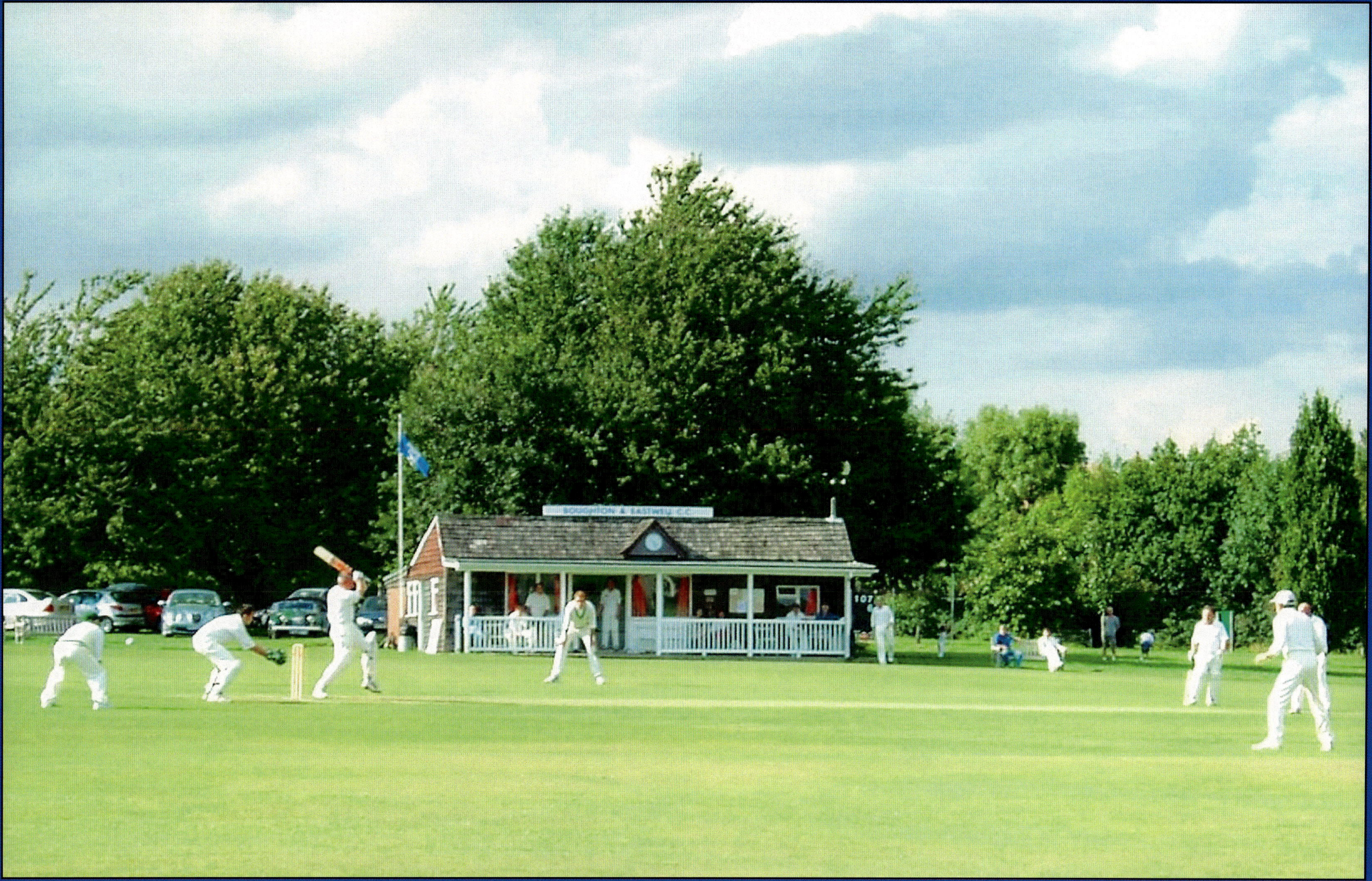

Photo by BJ Tritton

images **of Kent**

  Beach huts and golf course, Whitstable

Photo by Ron Ward

Photo by Phil Houghton

images of Kent

    The River Stour and Westgate Tower, Canterbury   Photo by Trevor Jefferies

 Views from woods behind Igtham Mote

Photo by Craig Davies

images of Kent

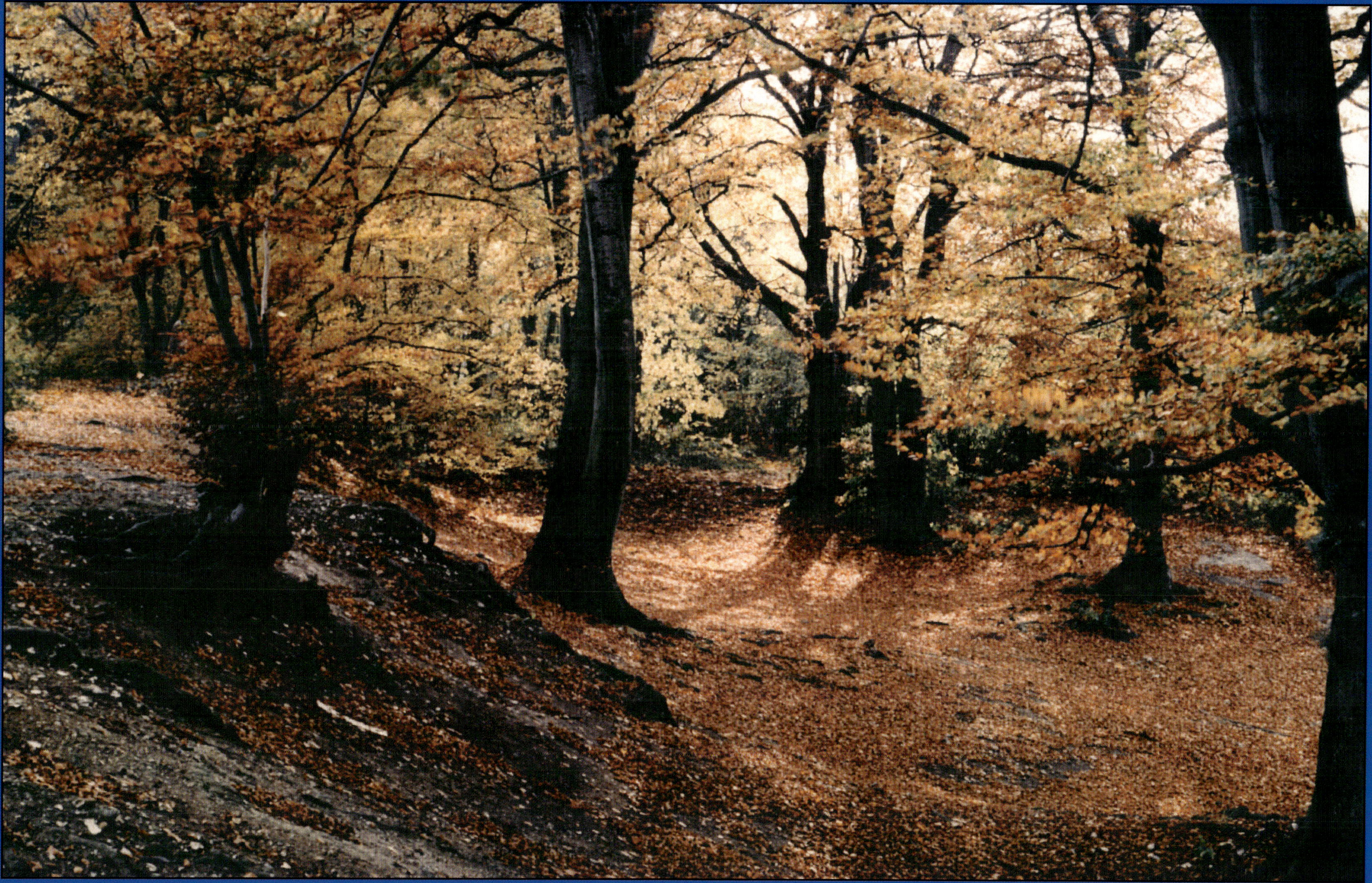

Photo by Arthur J Page FRPS

images of Kent

    St Margarets Bay, near Deal

Photo by Philip Drew

images **of Kent**

Photo by Eric Keys

images of Kent

Photo by Denis Johnson

   Yachts off the beach at Walmer

Photo by Eddie Reumel

  Kings Ferry Bridge

Photo by PJ Brook

images **of Kent**

Photo by Andrew Whittaker

images of Kent

 Sunset over the Swale at Queenborough, Isle of Sheppey   Photo by Martin Verrier

images **of Kent**

Photo by Richard Foster

images of Kent

Photo by Richard Fraser

images of Kent

Photo by AP Friend

Photo by Phil Houghton

Photo by P Melia

images **of Kent**

    Russell Gardens, Kearsney

Photo by Karol Steele

Photo by Phil Houghton

images of Kent

Photo by Damon Nielsen

images of Kent

Photo by ML Arrowsmith

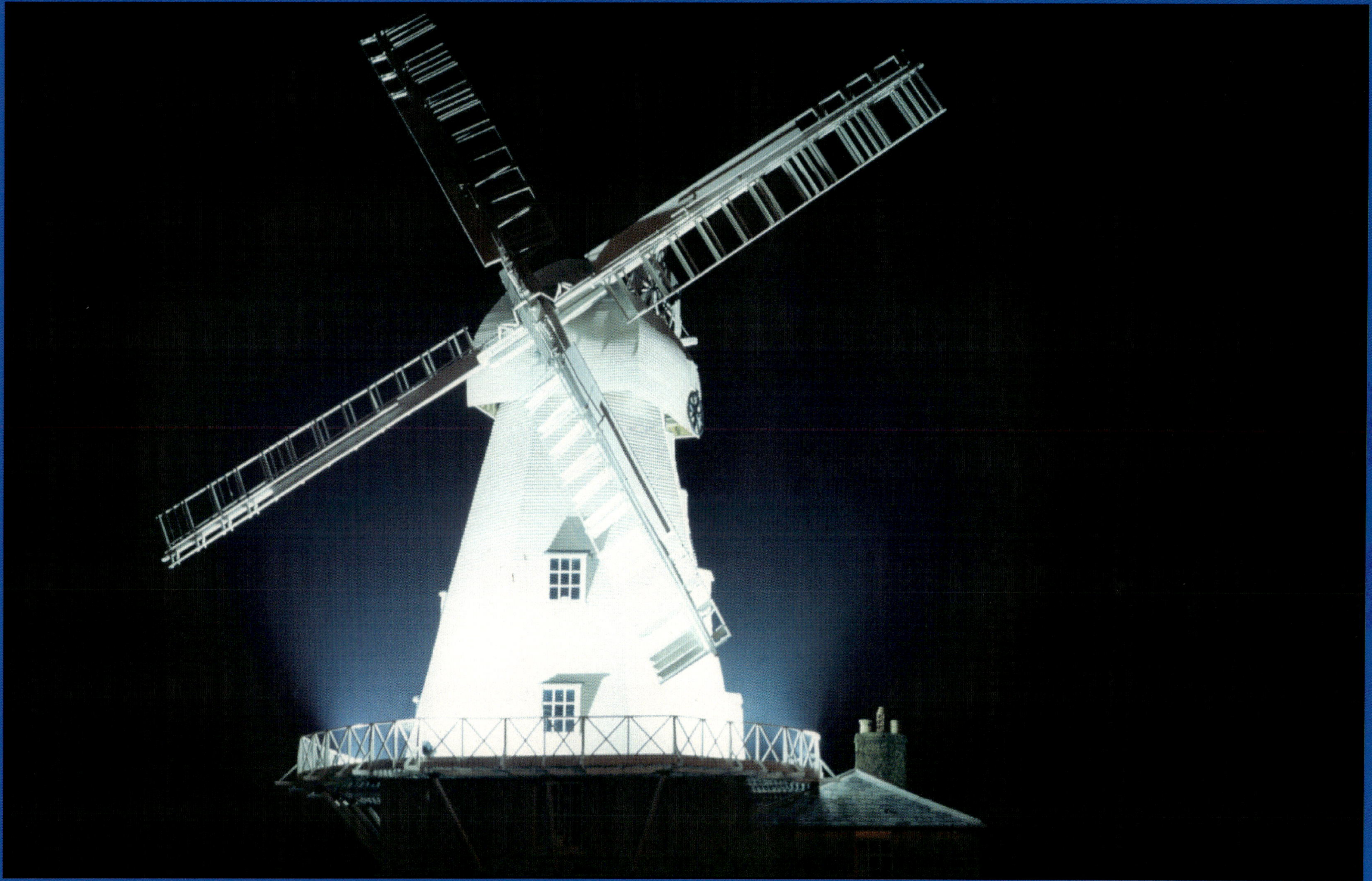

91 Willesborough Windmill Photo by Ian Feather

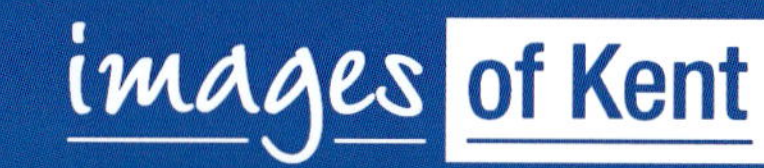

Photo by Phil Houghton

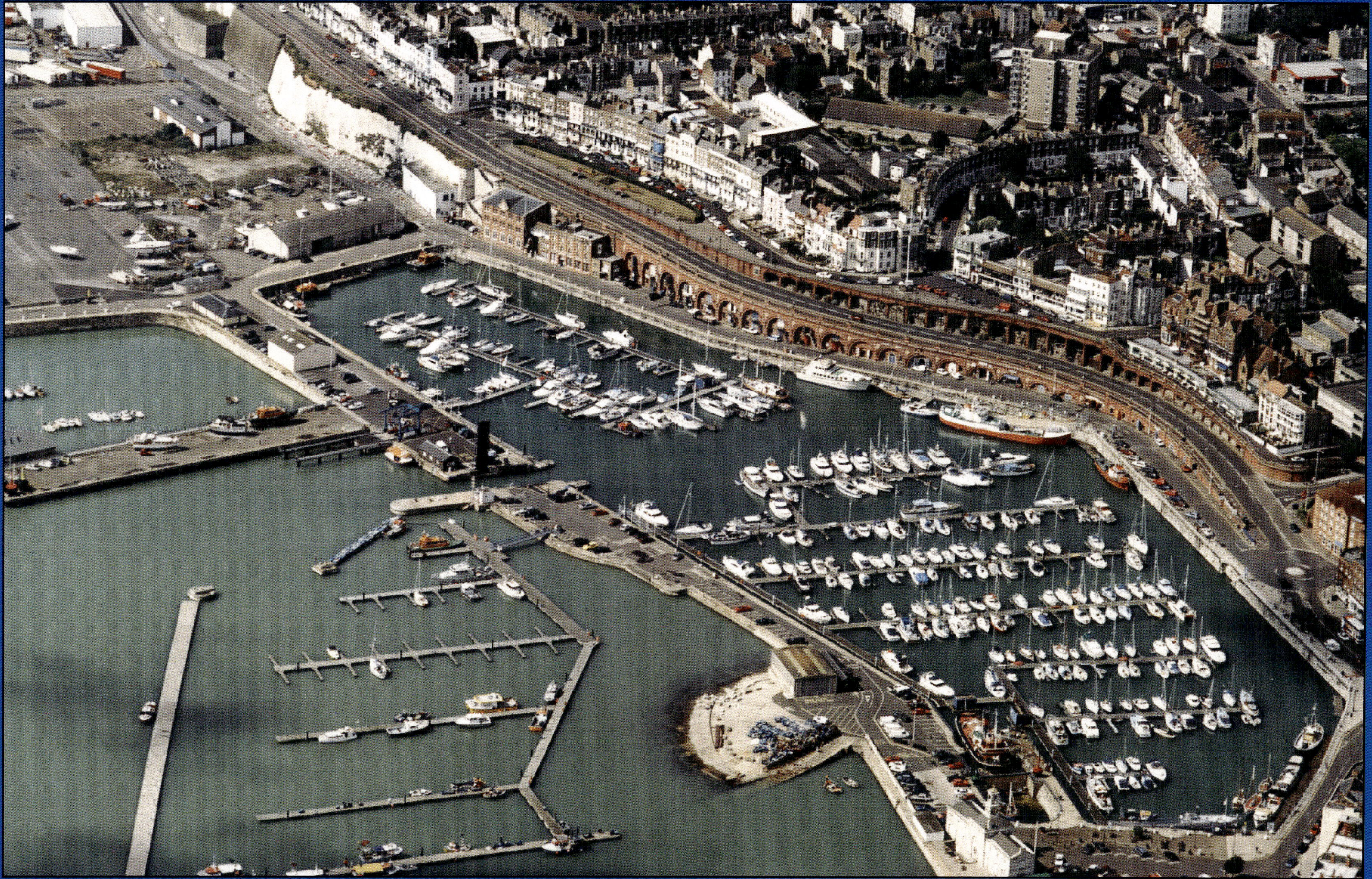

Photo by David Bowie

images of Kent

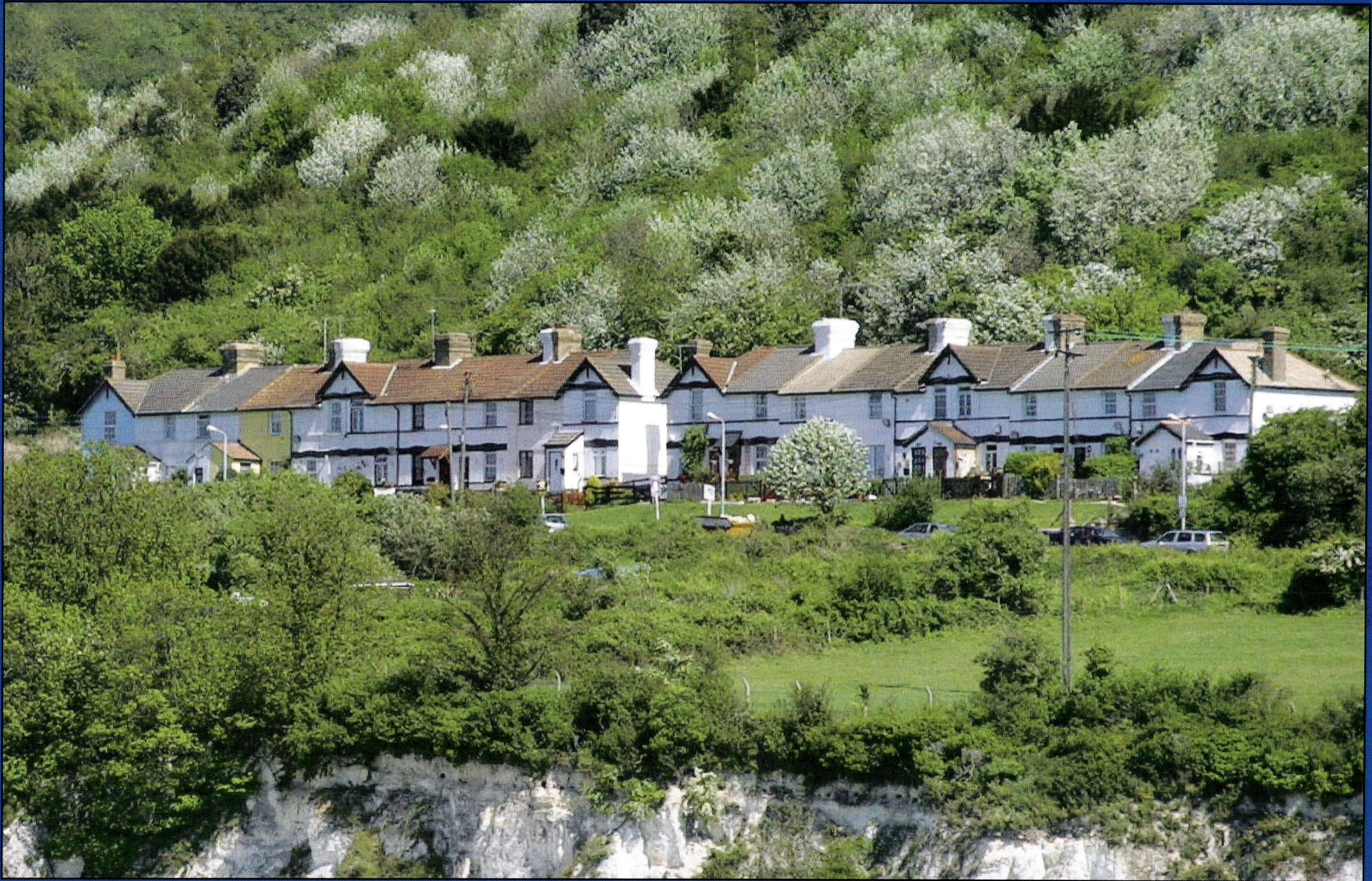

Photo by Keith Thompson

Photo by Phil Houghton

images of Kent

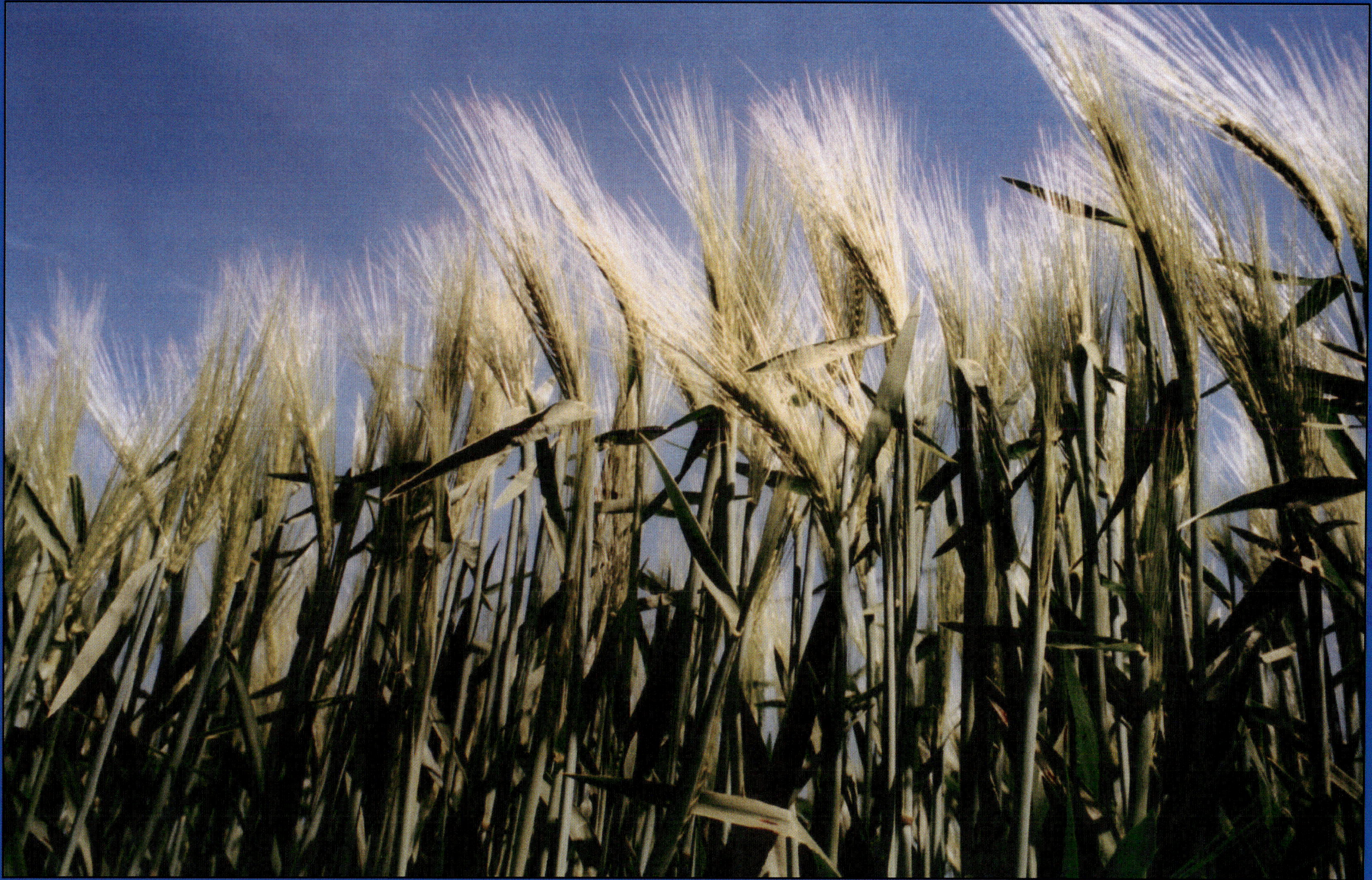

  Barley Field, Darenth

Photo by Christopher Allison

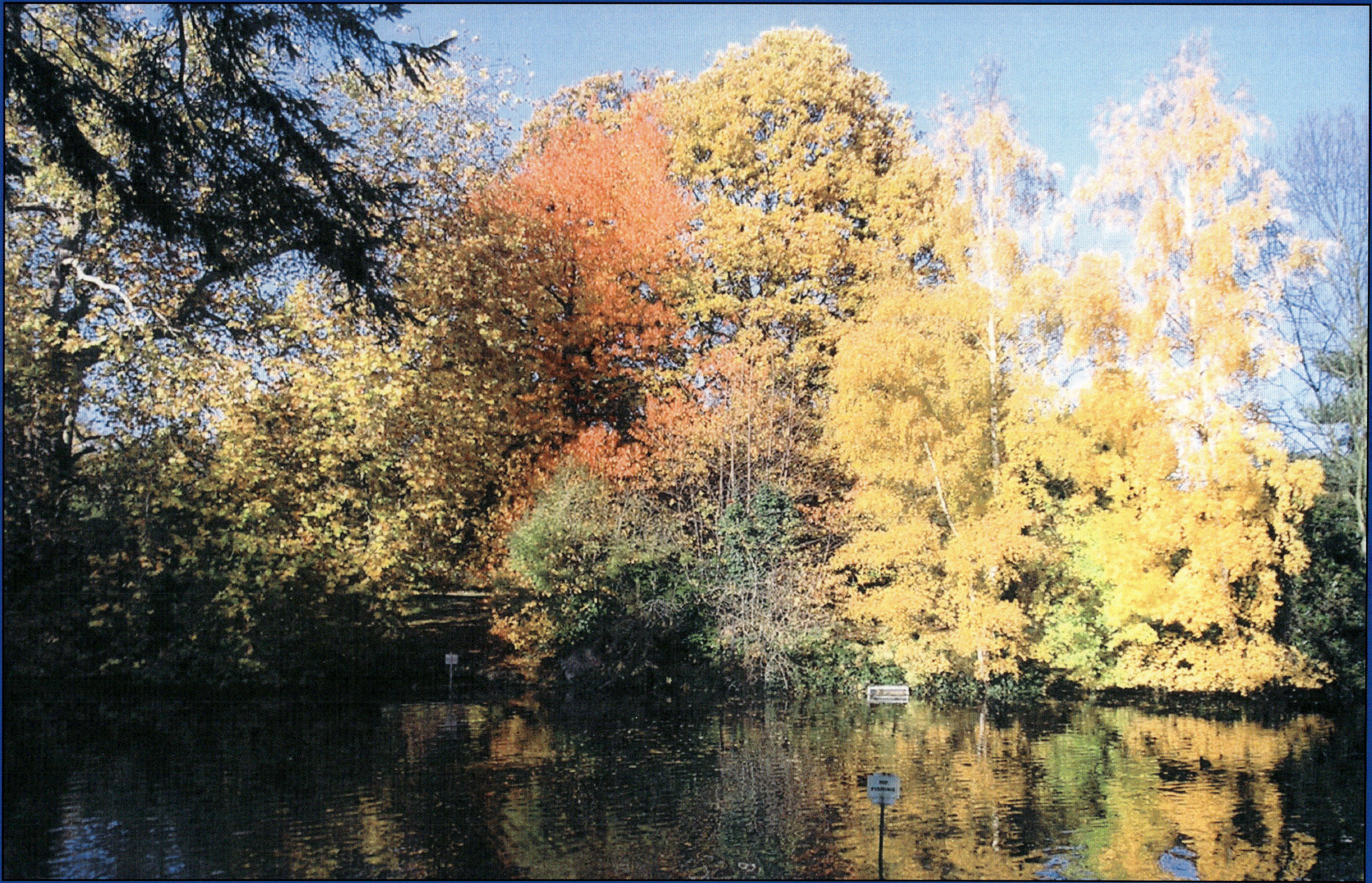

Photo by CA Ratcliff

images **of Kent**

Photo by Ron Ward

images of Kent

 Seasalter, Whitstable

Photo by John Pearson

Photo by Phil Houghton

images **of Kent**

 South Darenth, near Dartford

Photo by Lynn Hill

images of Kent

Photo by Mary Alwood

 Kingswear Castle paddle steamer on the River Medway

Photo by John Hunt

images of Kent

    Battle of Britain memorial, Folkestone   Photo by TB Clark   *images* **of Kent**

Photo by Craig Semphis

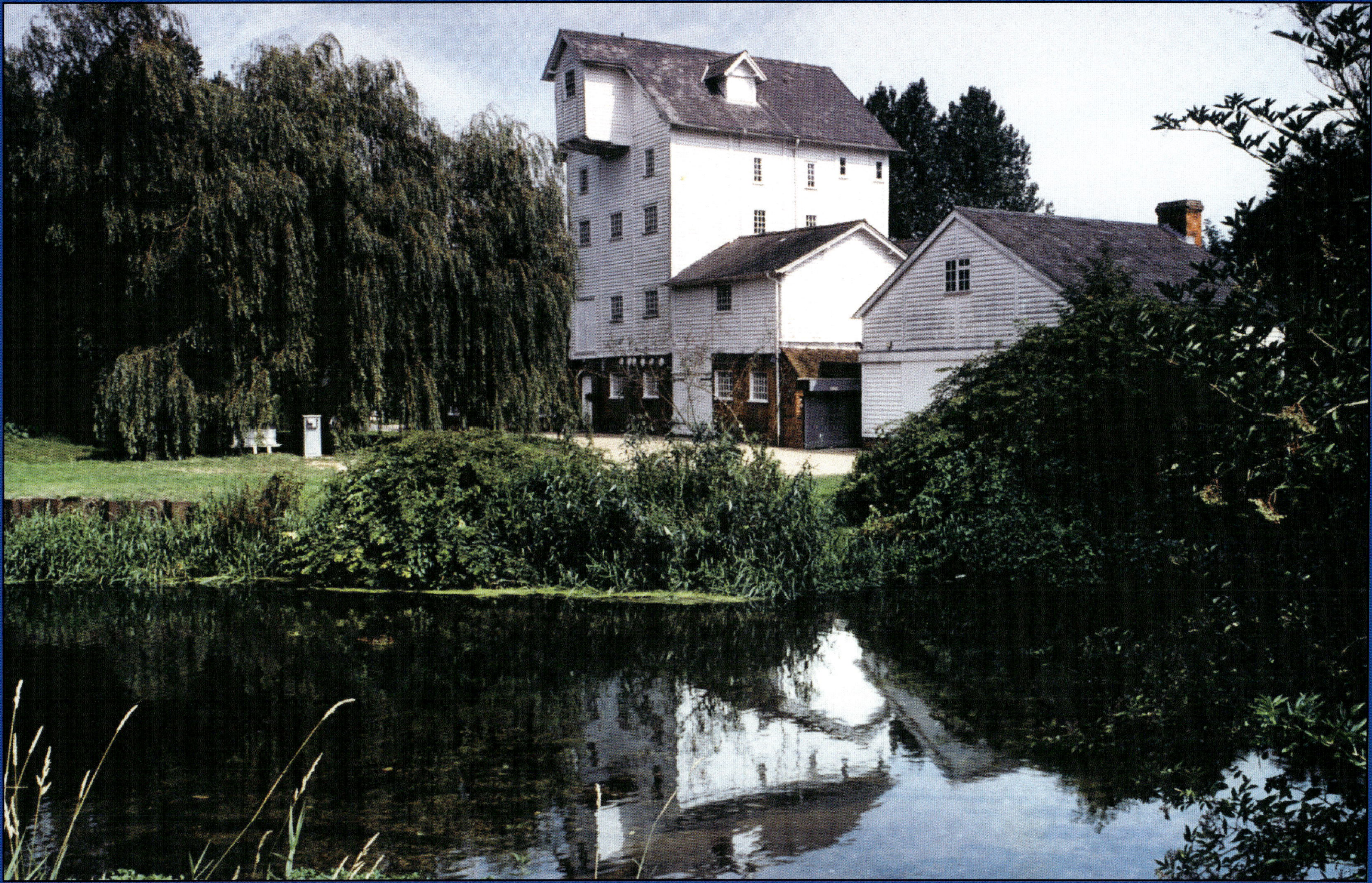

Photo by Arthur J Page FRPS

Photo by EP Ashdown

Photo by Keith Thompson

images **of Kent**

   St Mary's Island, Chatham

Photo by Andrew Whittaker

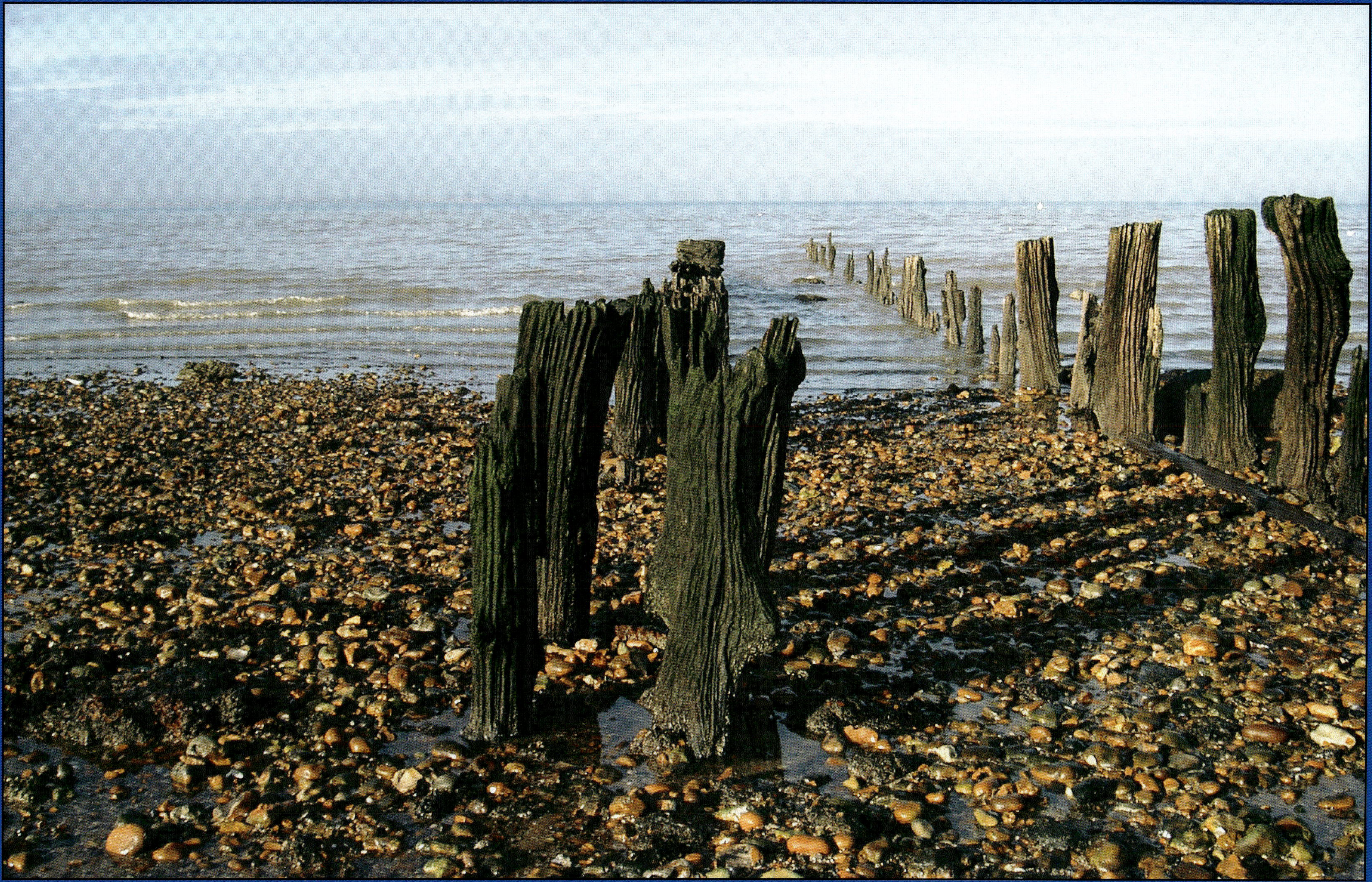

   Groynes along the shore, Whitstable

Photo by Martin Boa

    Hythe Imperial Hotel, Hythe

Photo by Philip Drew

images **of Kent**

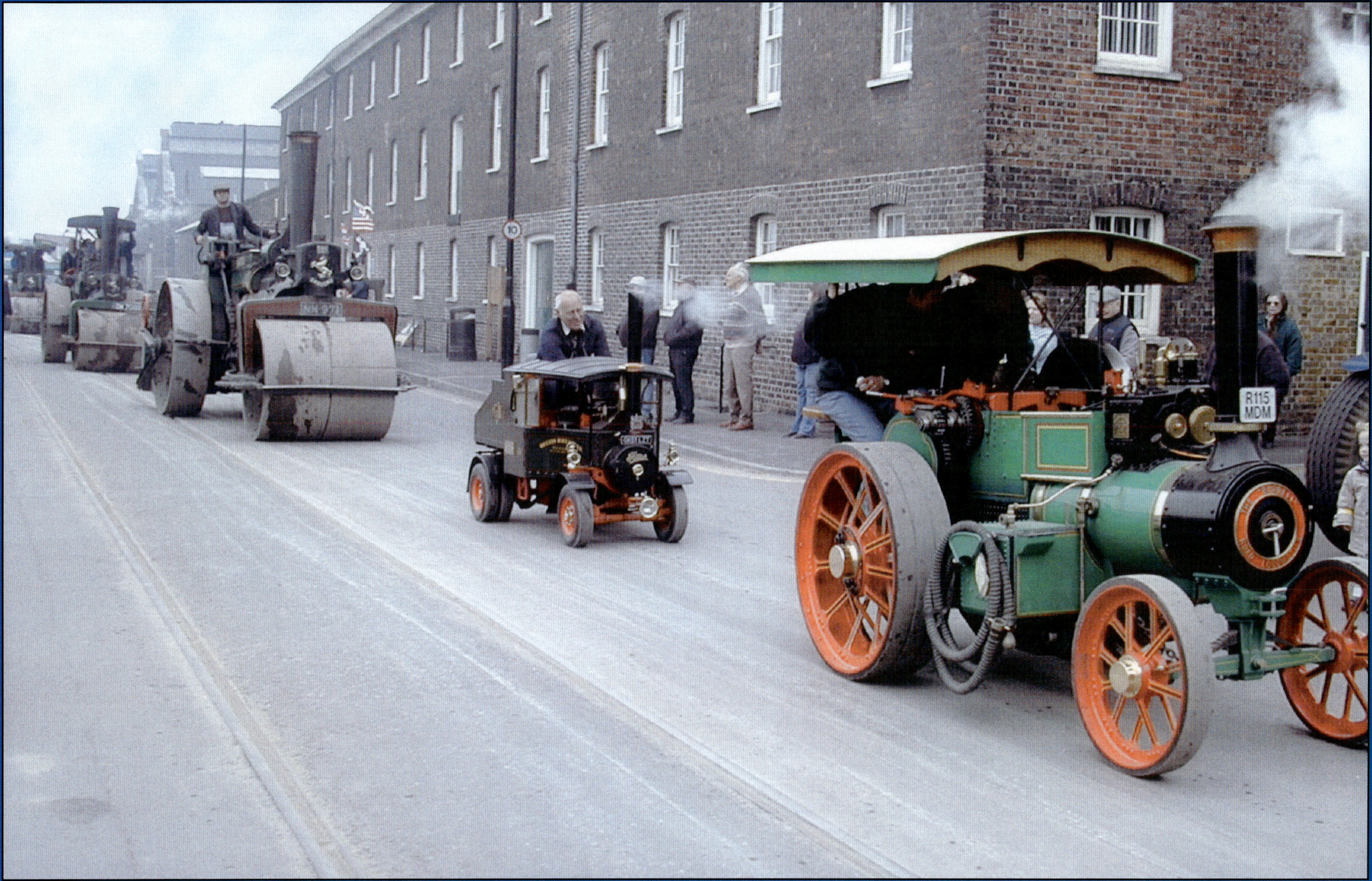

   Medway Festival of Steam and Transport at the Historic Dockyard, Chatham   Photo by WH Bailey

Photo by Phil Houghton

images of Kent

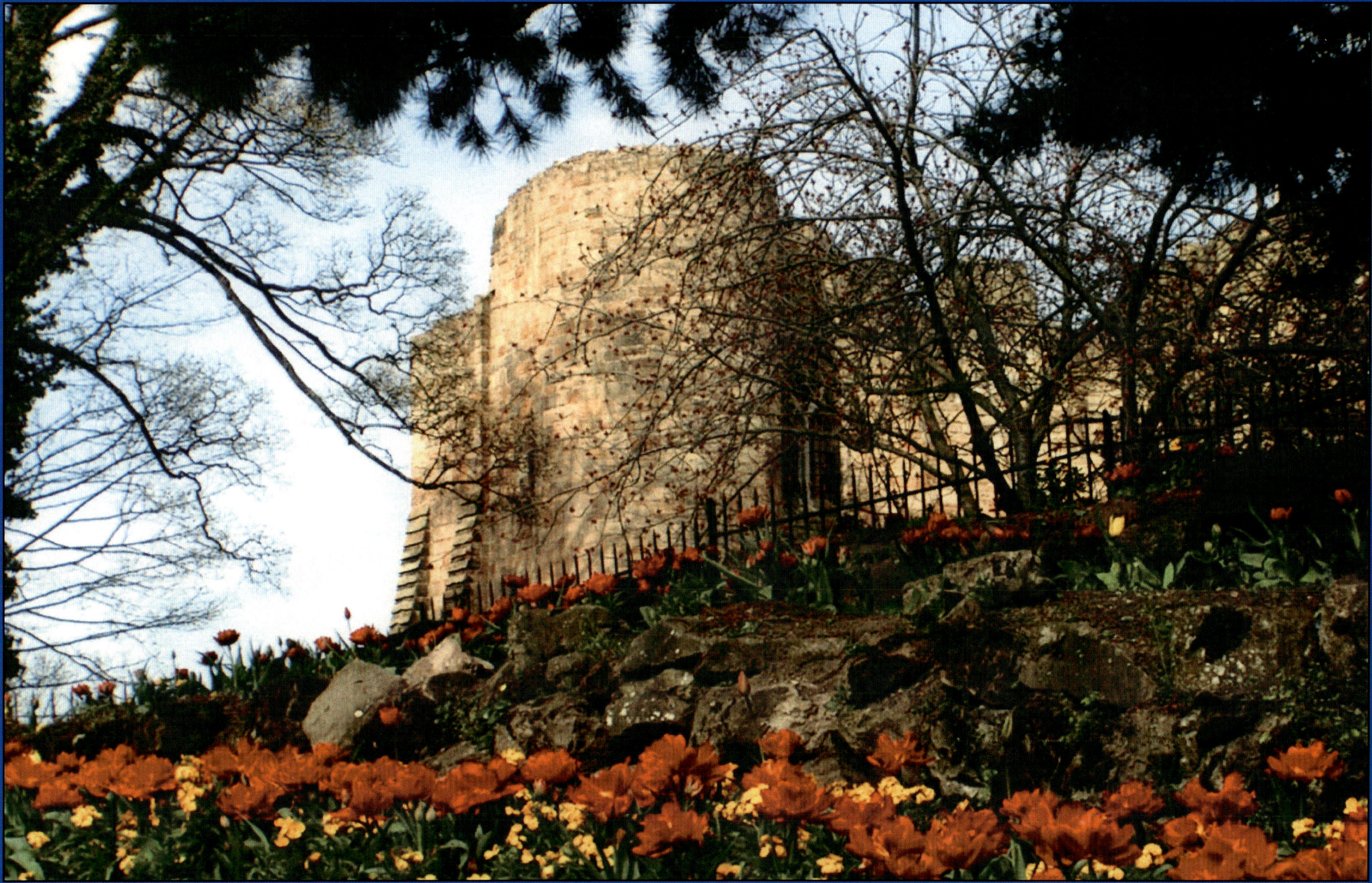

Photo by Craig Davies

images **of Kent**

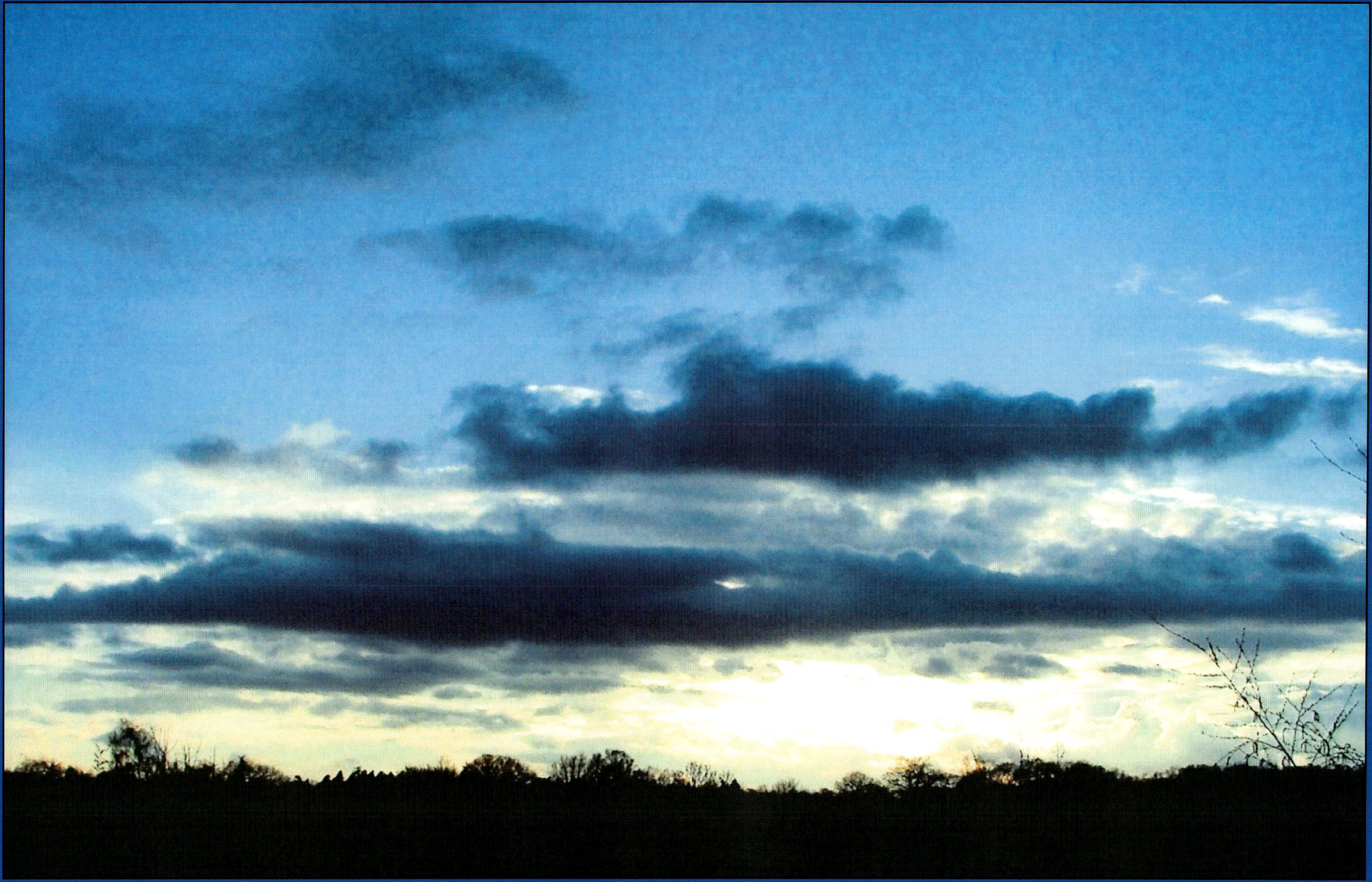

Photo by Neil Rutherfoord

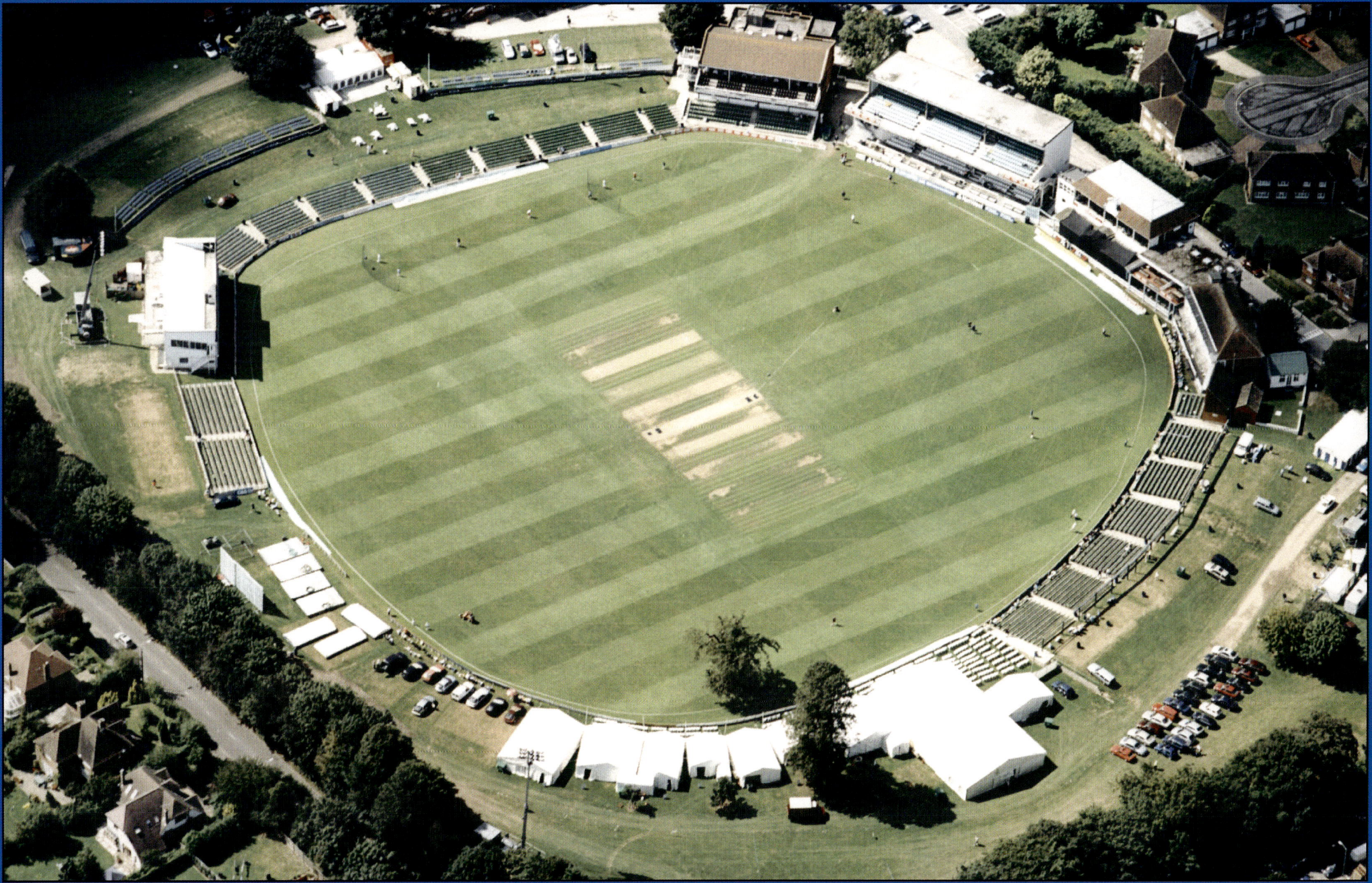

   St Lawrence cricket ground, Canterbury   Photo by David Bowie

Photo by Phil Houghton

South Foreland Lighthouse, St Margarets, near Dover

Photo by Robert Scarfe

images **of Kent**

Photo by Richard Ashbee

images of Kent

Photo by Phil Houghton

Photo by Damon Nielsen

images **of Kent**

Photo by Andrew Burger

images of Kent

  Fishing Boat

Photo by Phil Houghton

images of Kent

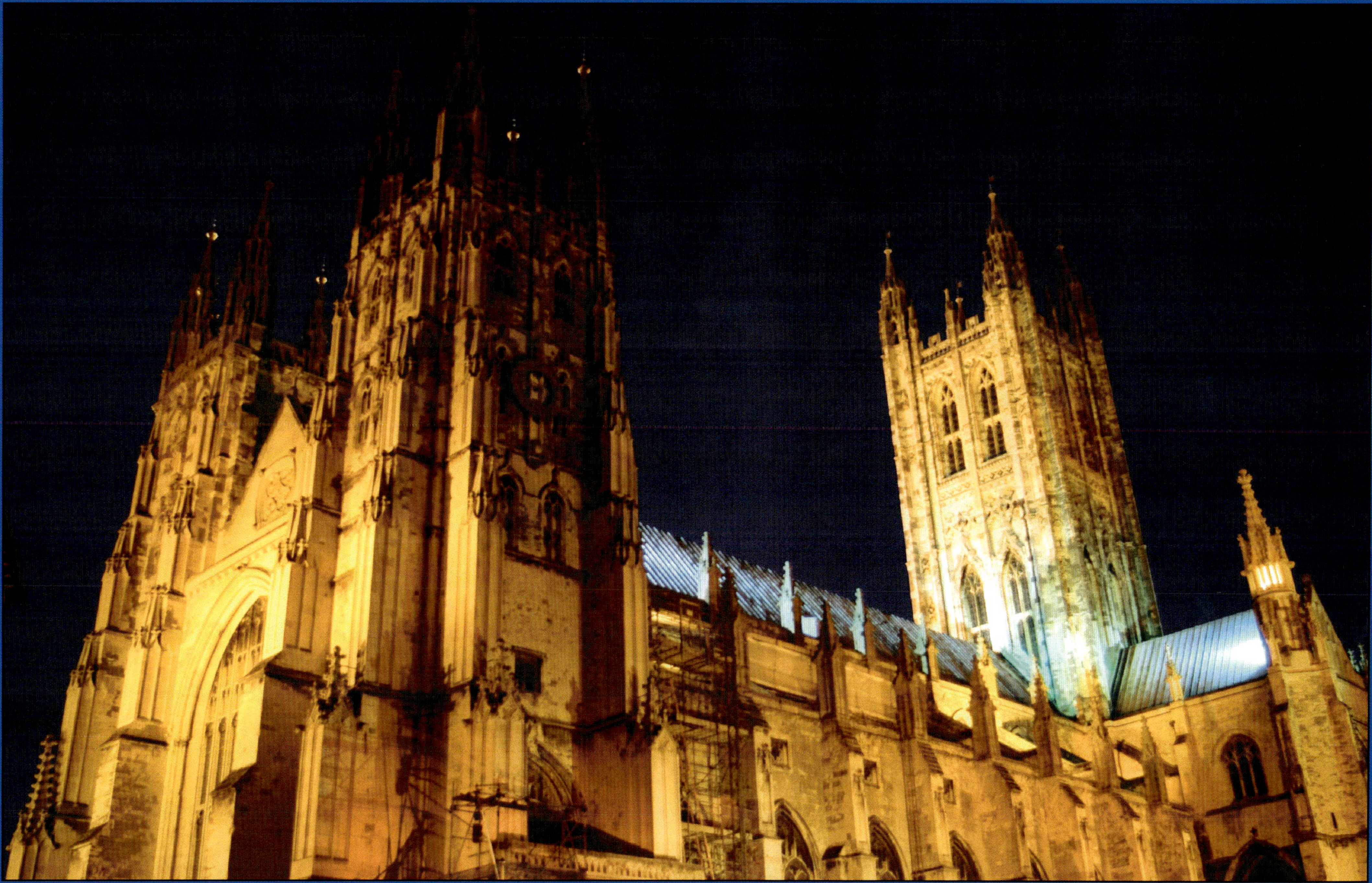

157 Canterbury Cathedral

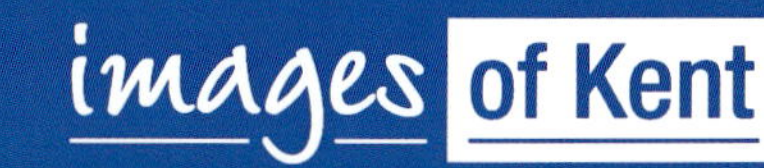

Photo by P Melia

Photo by DE Sims

Photo by Denis Johnson

images of Kent

Photo by Keith Thompson

images of Kent

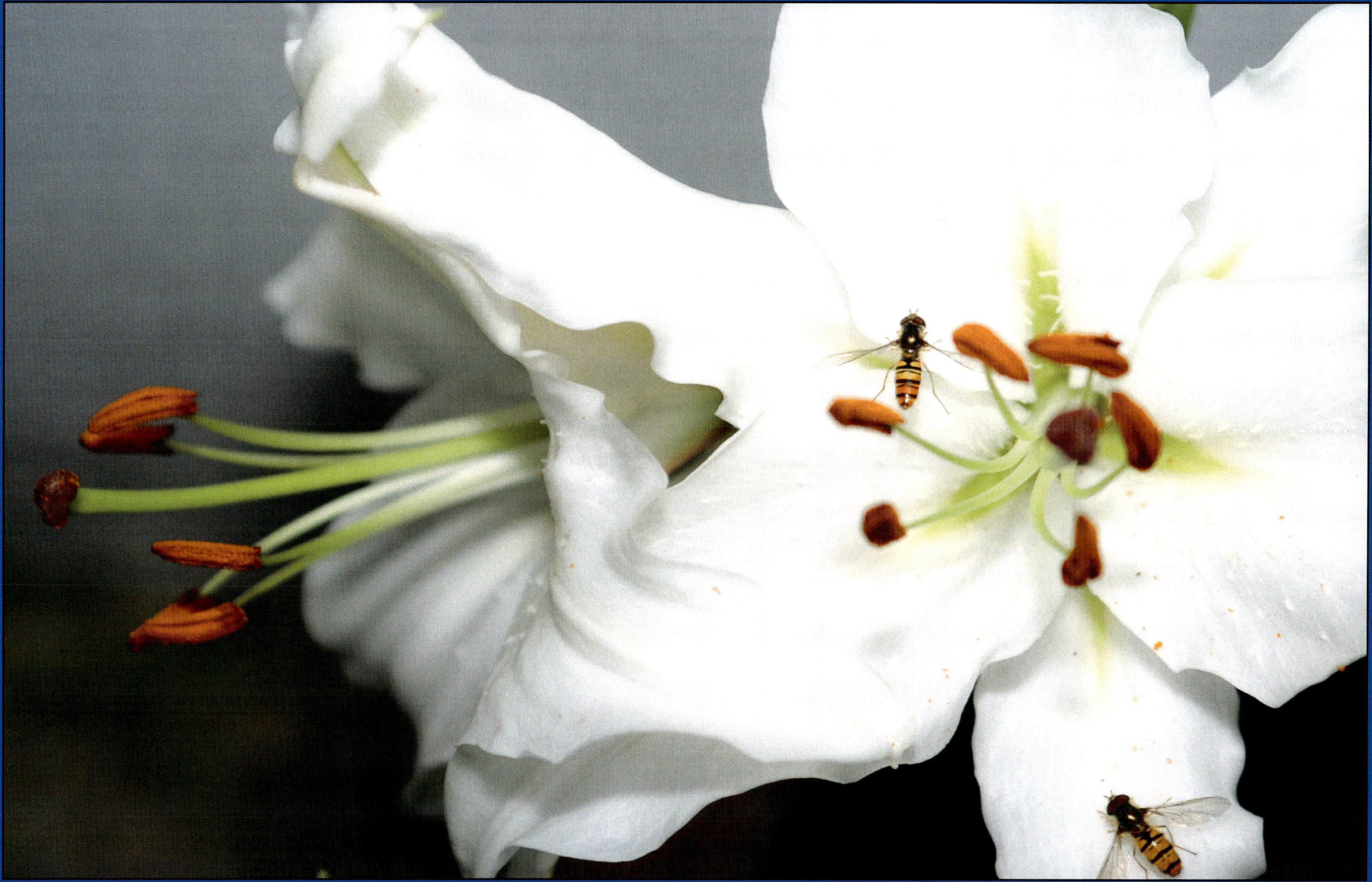

Photo by Phil Houghton

images of Kent

Photo by Jo Scott

Photo by Richard Foster

images of Kent

    Ripple Windmill in a field of rape

Photo by Karol Steele

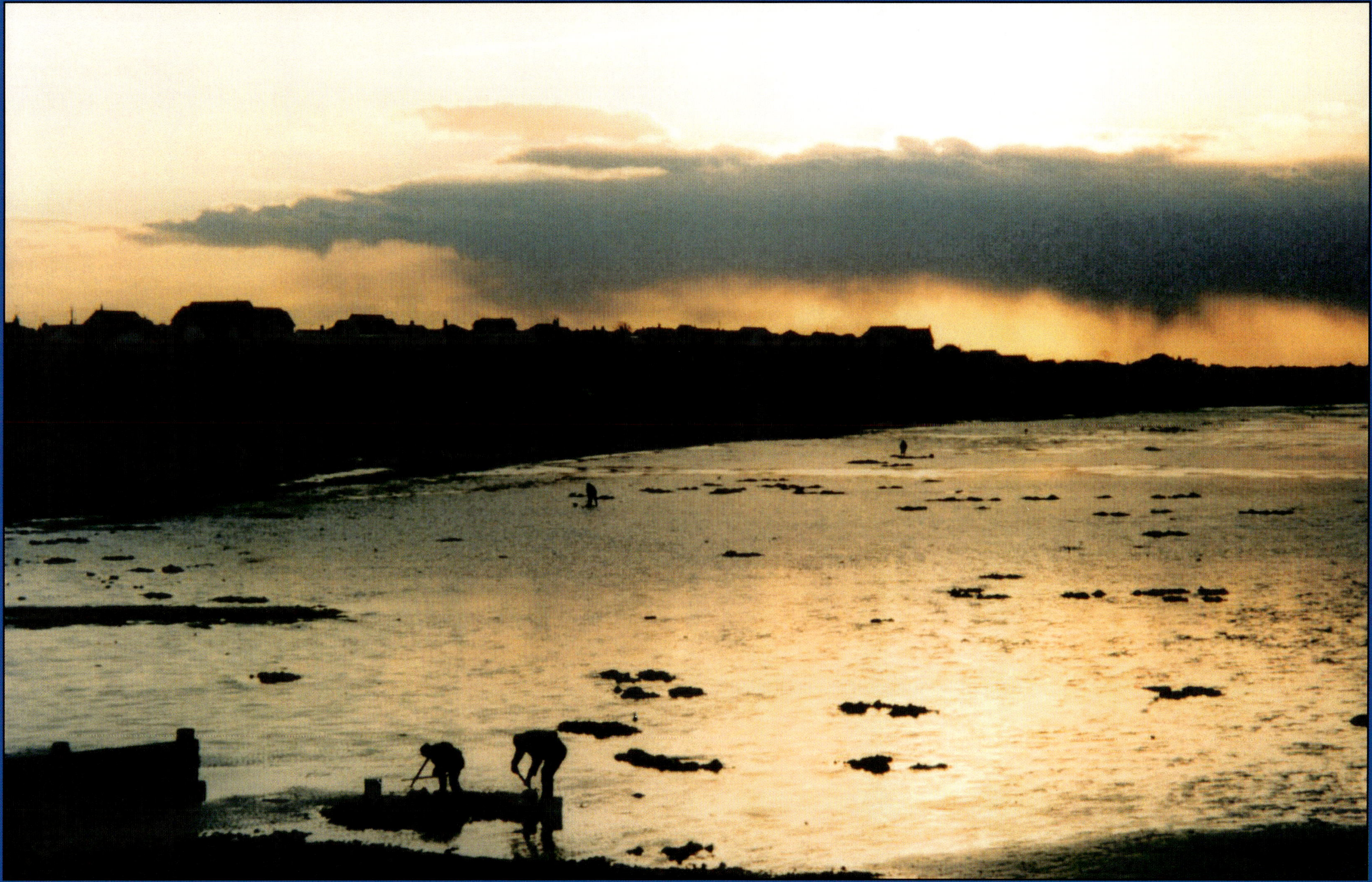

 Bait diggers, Hampton

Photo by Julia Geeves

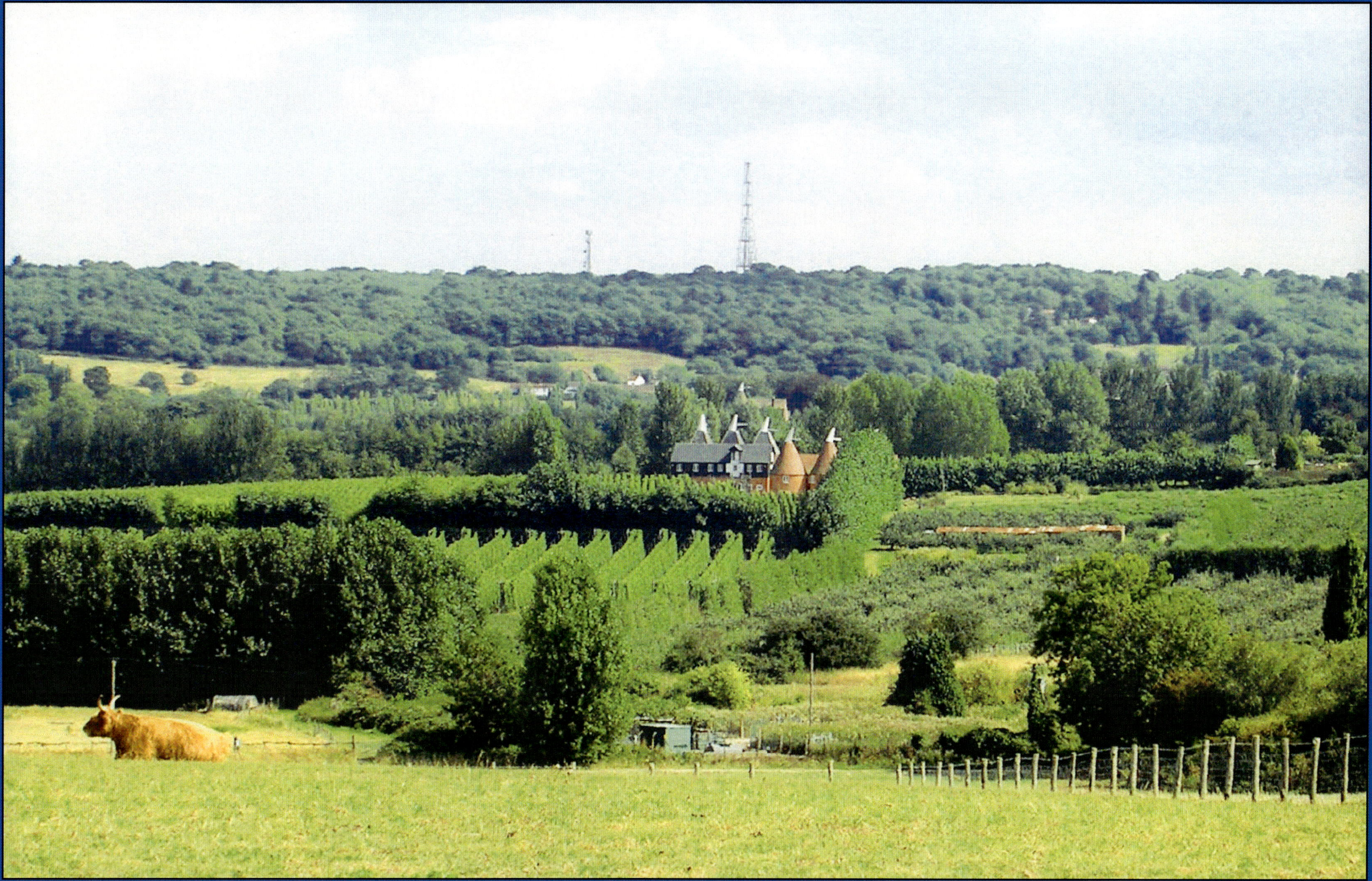

Photo by Lynn Whittington

images of Kent

Photo Barbara Macpherson

images of Kent

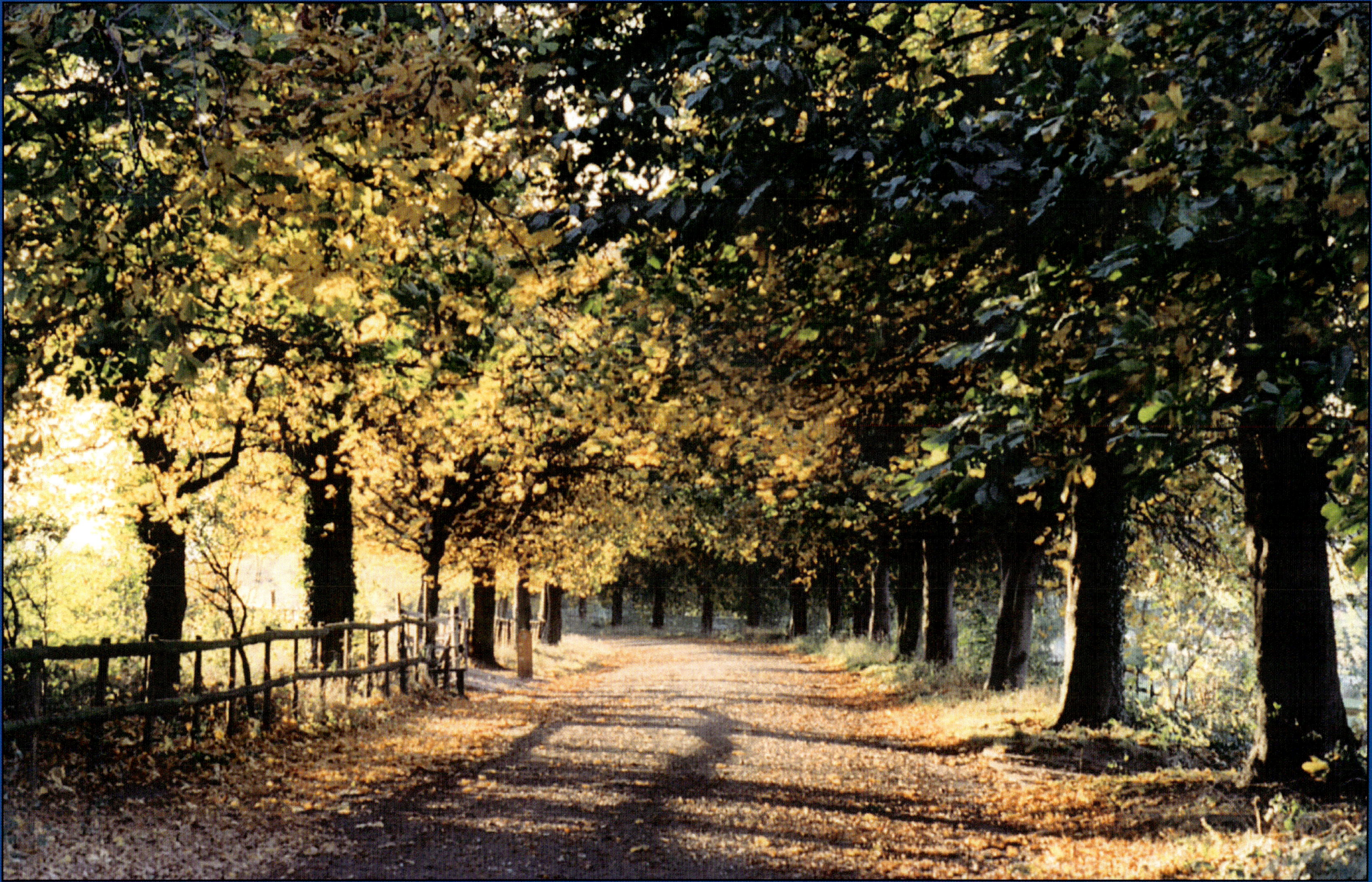

   Darenth Country Park

Photo V Coney

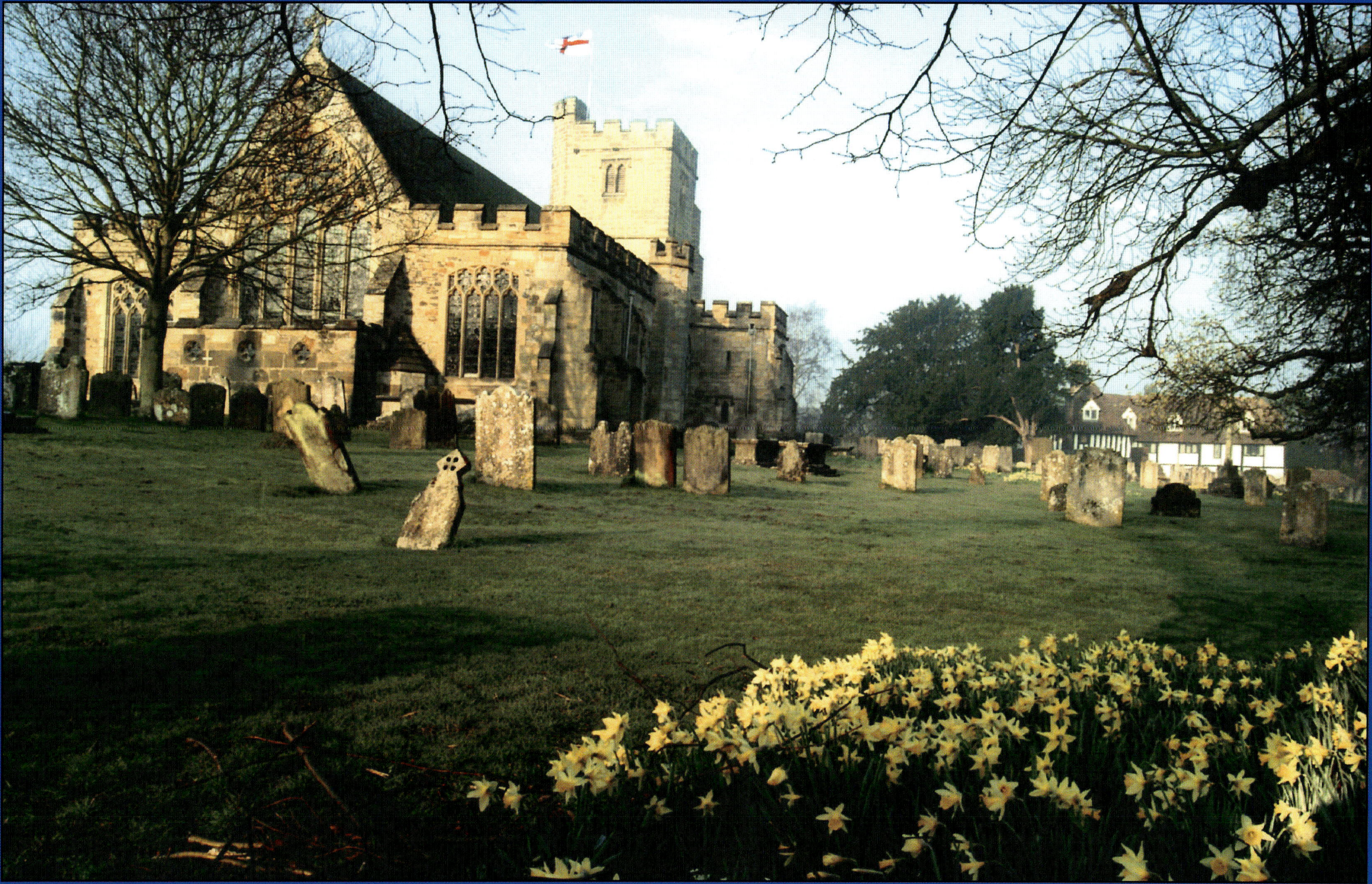

   St Laurance Church, Hawkhurst

Photo by John Hunt

    River Medway above the lock at Allington

Photo by Edward Field

images **of Kent**

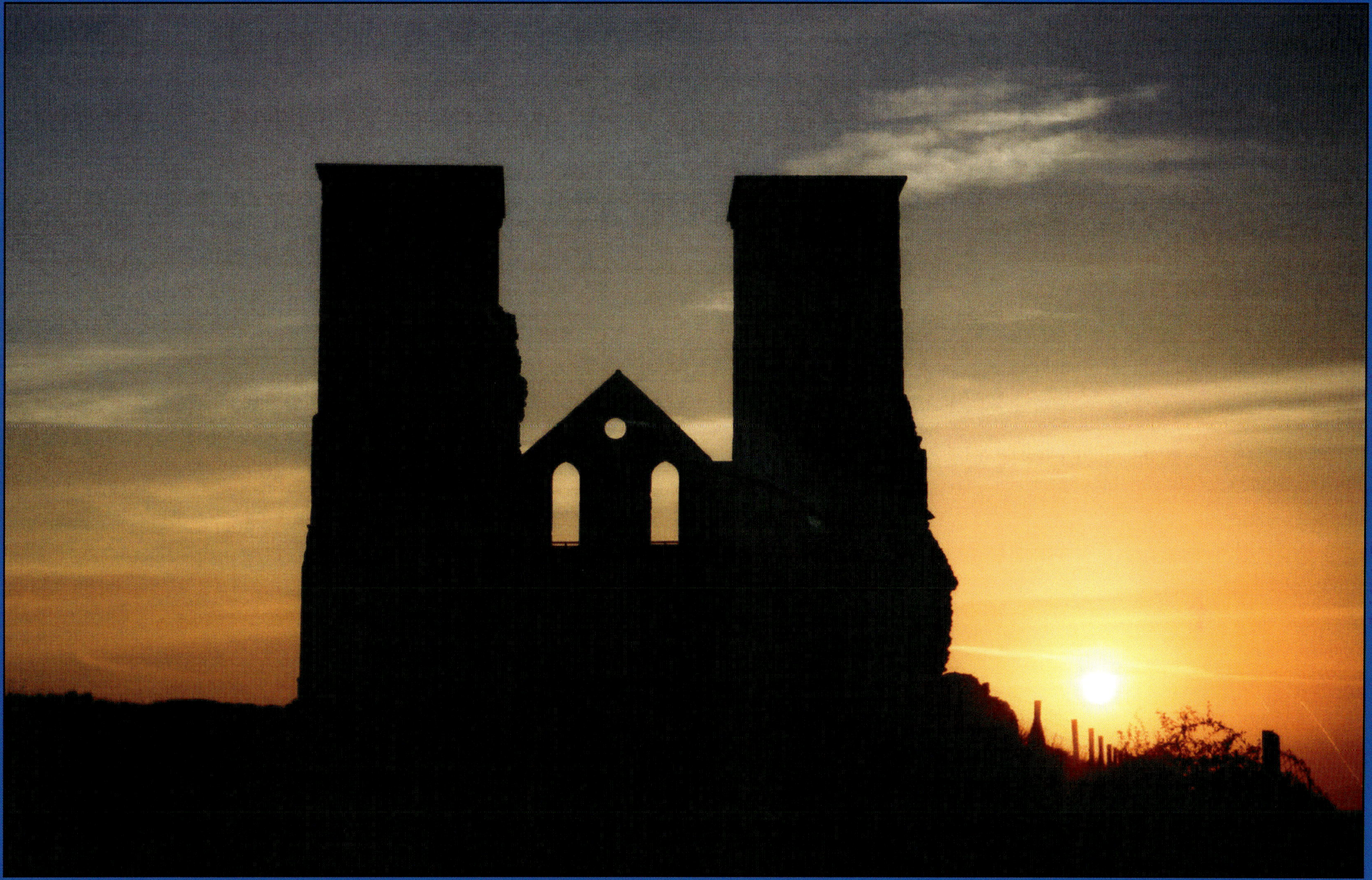

Photo by John Tapsell

images **of Kent**

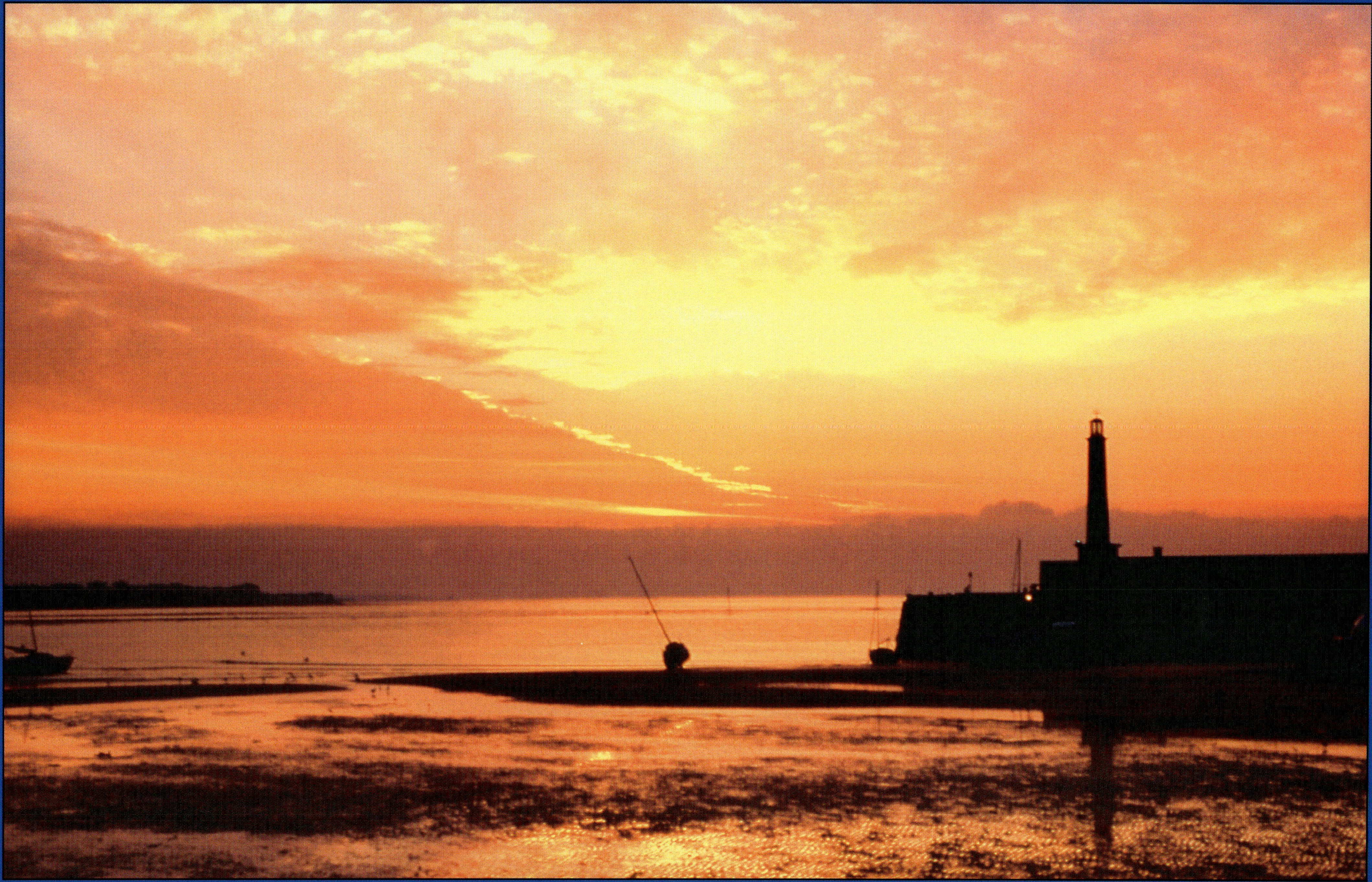

187 Margate Harbour

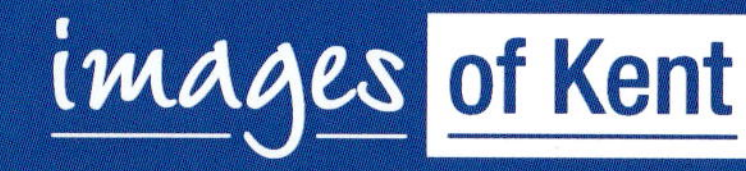

Photo by David Harris

images of Kent

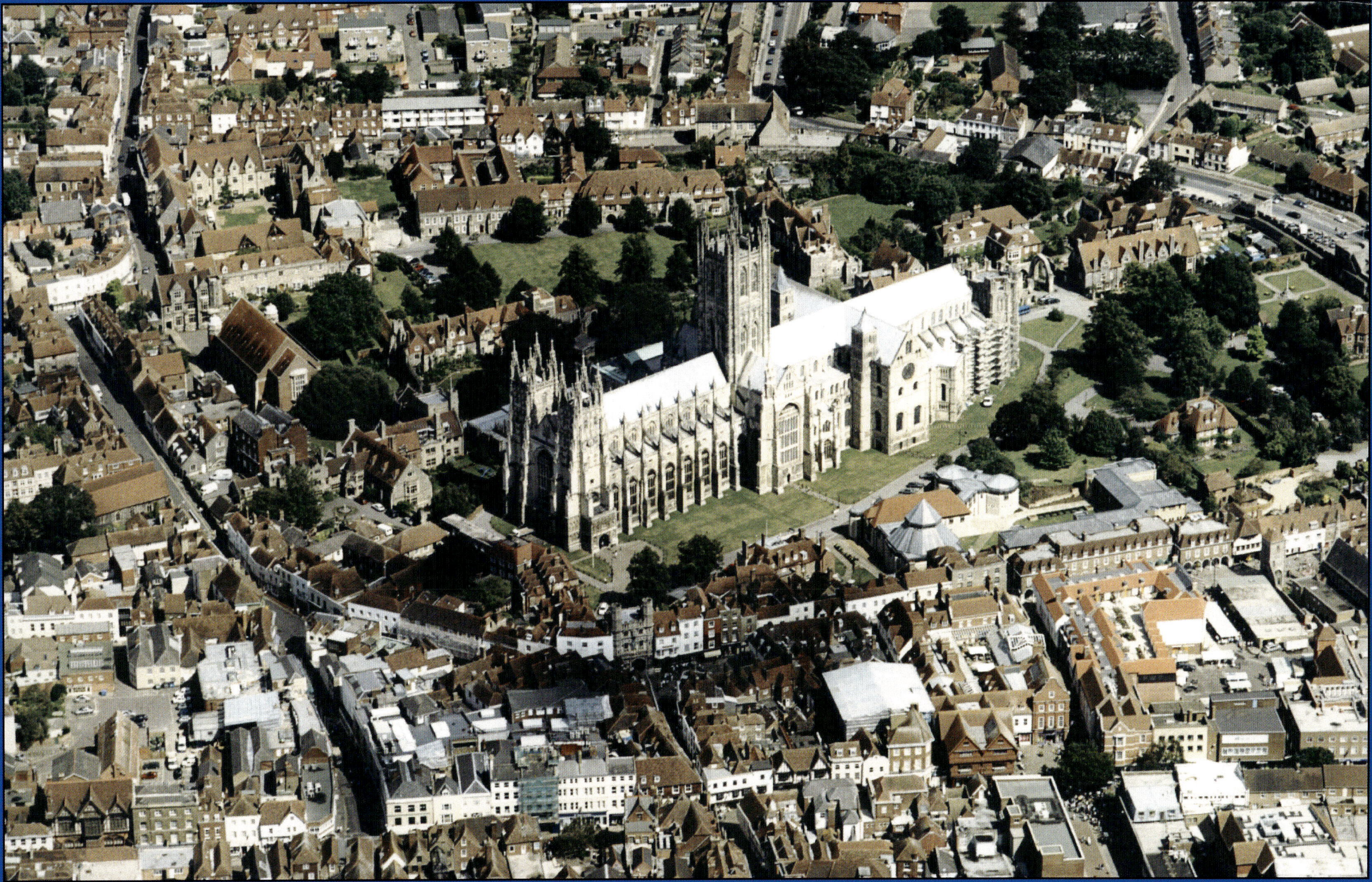

Photo by David Bowie

images **of Kent**

Photo by Colin Miles

 Chartwell, former home of Winston Churchill

Photo by Phil Bland

images **of Kent**

Photo by CA O'Brien

images **of Kent**

Photo by Phil Houghton

images **of Kent**

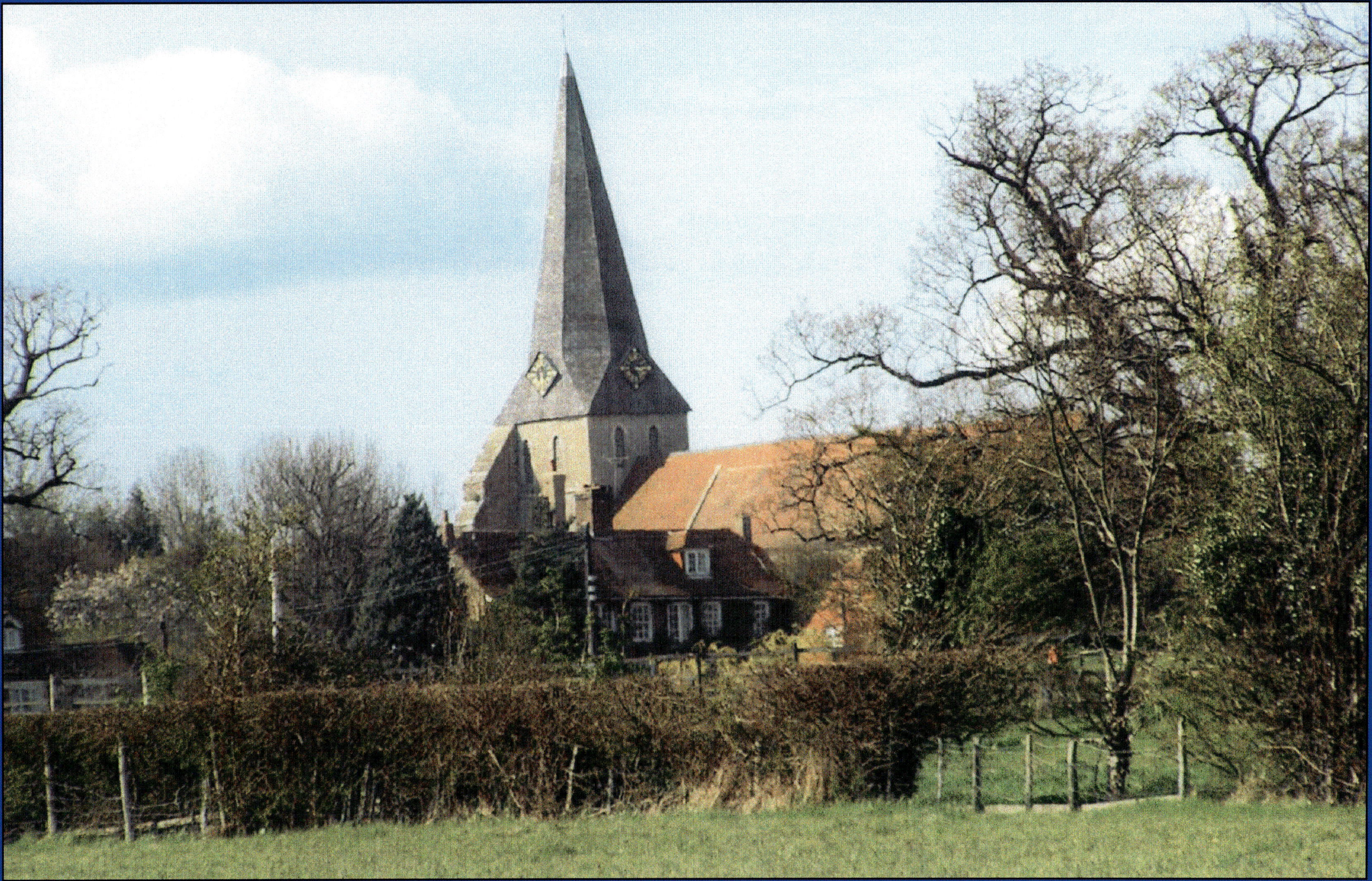

Photo by John Pellett

images of Kent

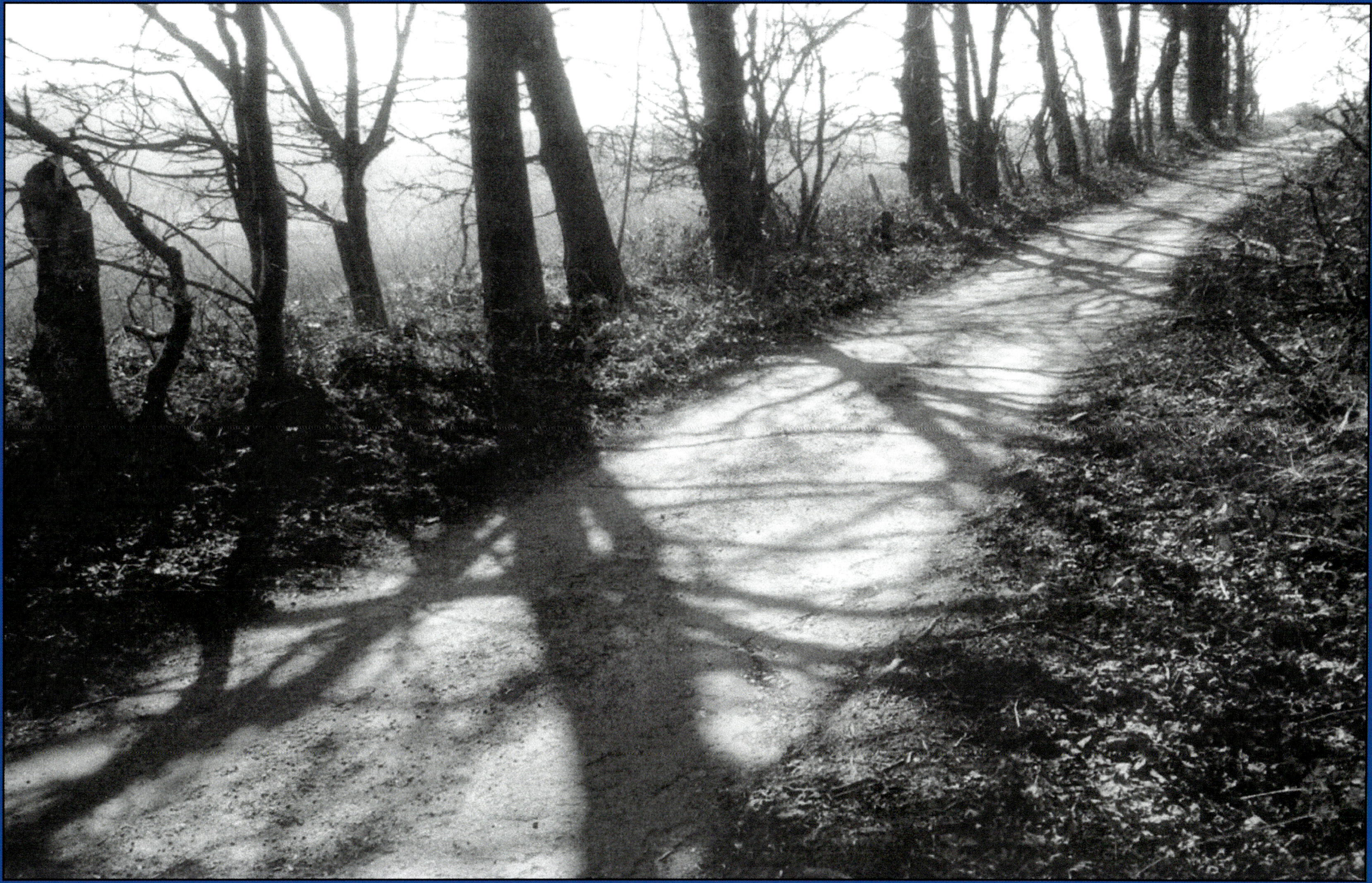

Photo by Christopher Allison

Photo by Ron Ward

images of Kent

 Looking over Blean Woods, Canterbury

Photo by Neil Rutherfoord

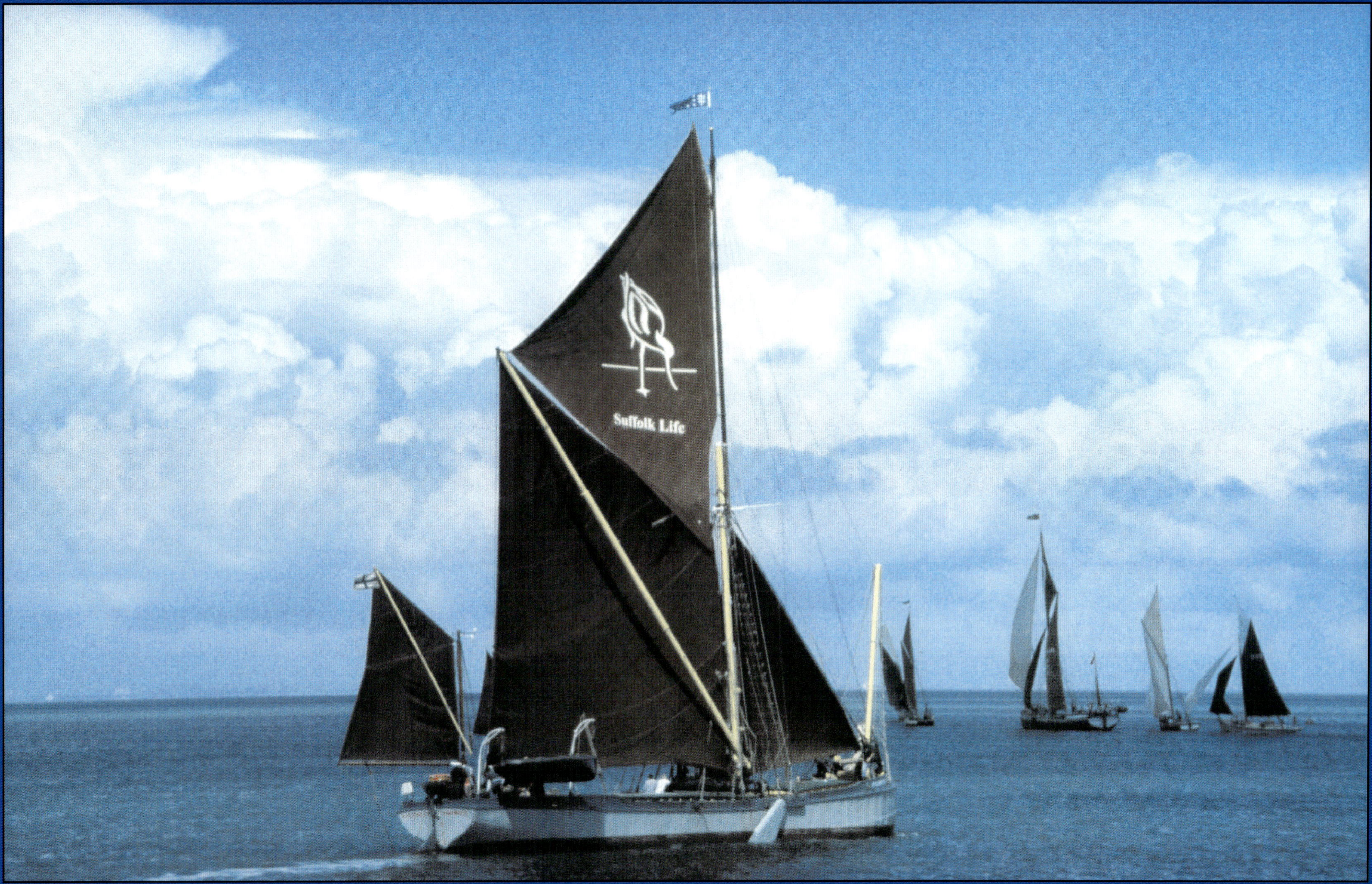

Photo by Denise Etheridge

images of Kent

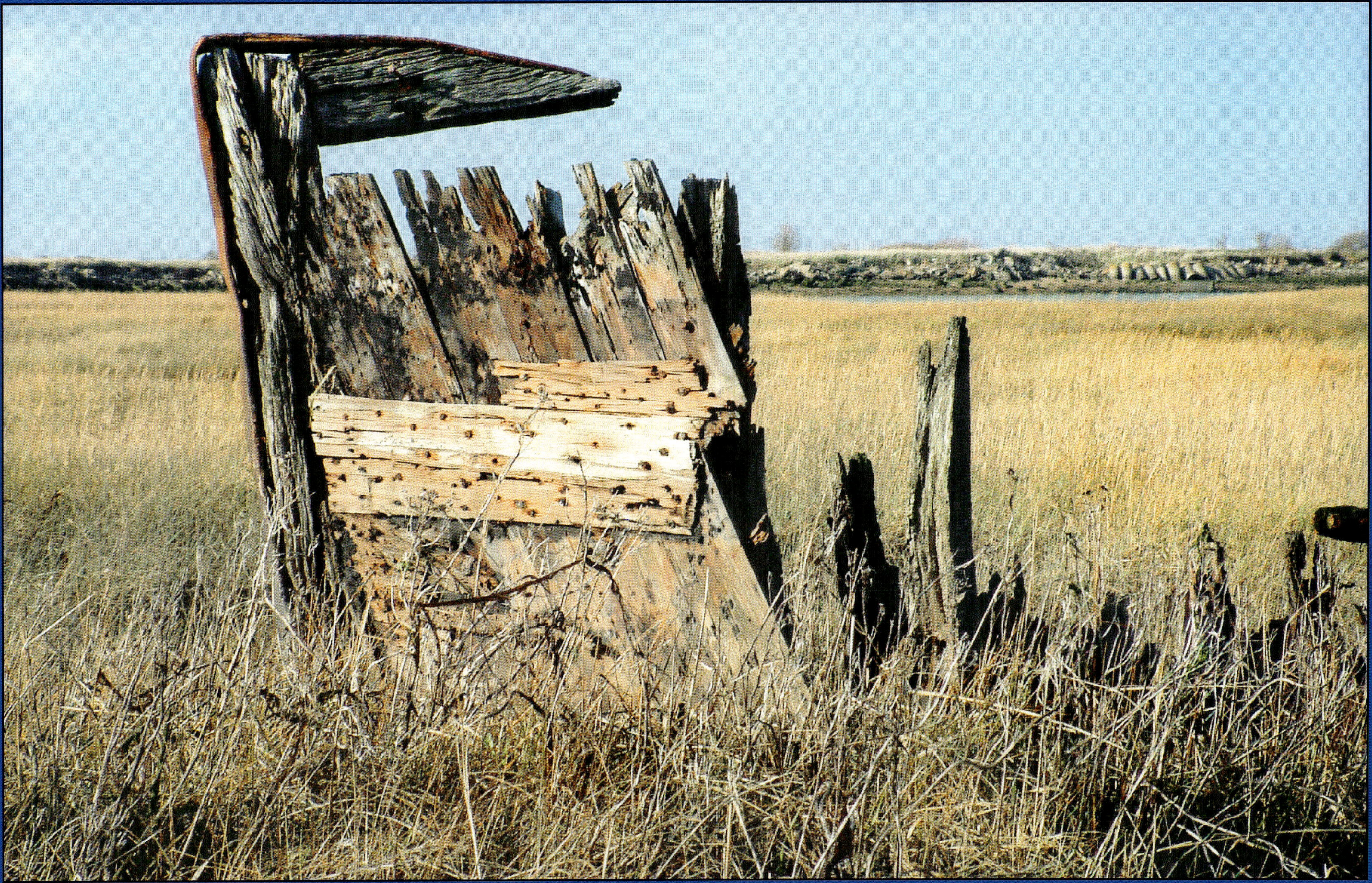

Photo by Den Johnson

images **of Kent**

Photo by Phil Houghton

images **of Kent**

 Langton Cliffs, Dover

Photo by Richard Varrall

    The renovated Gravesend pier

Photo by Andrew Whittaker

images **of Kent**

Photo by Phil Houghton

images of Kent

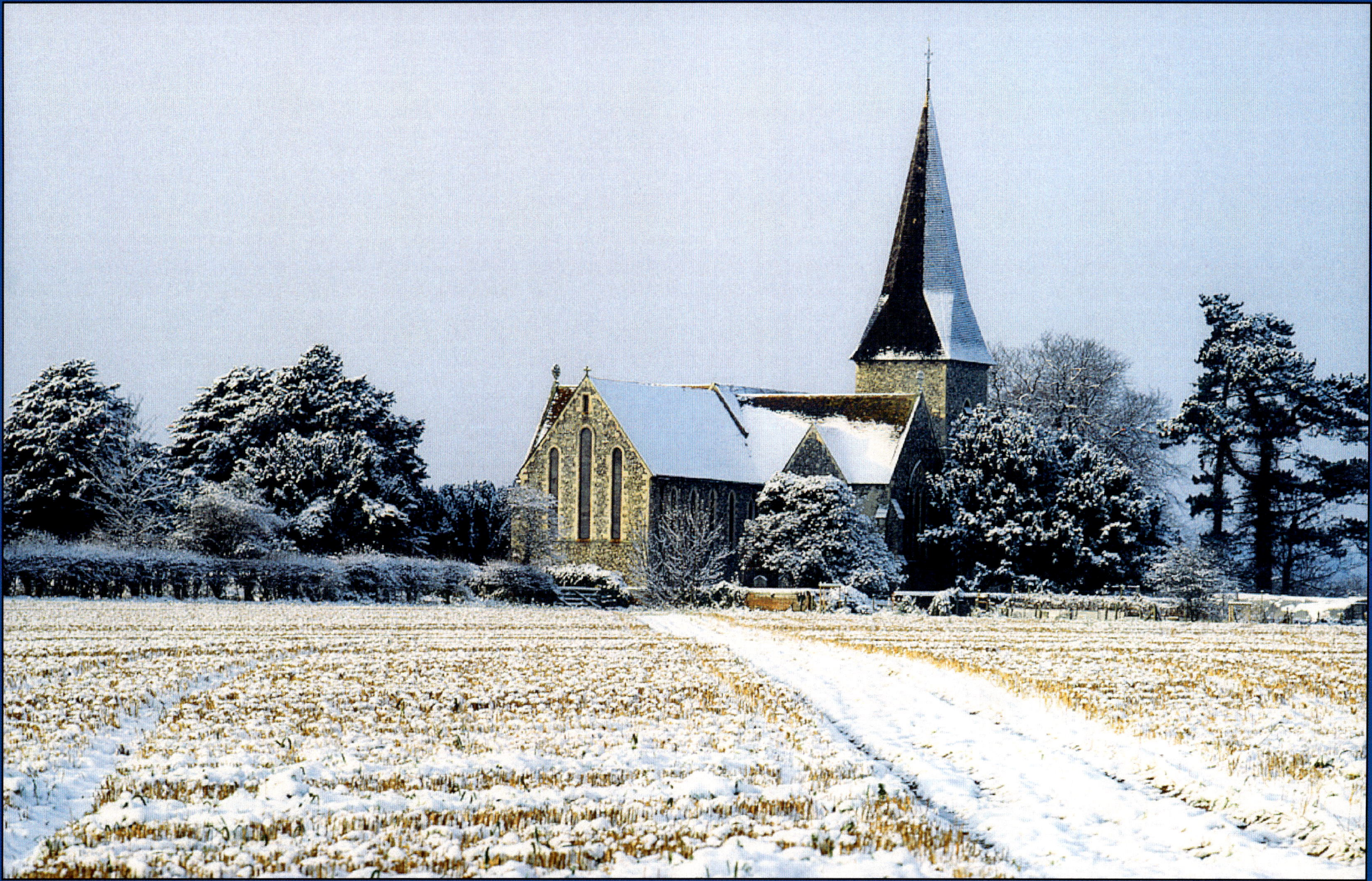

   St John's, Ickham, near Canterbury

Photo by Major Steadman

Photo by Hugh Dolding

images of Kent

Photo by Damon Nielsen

Photo by Phil Houghton

images of Kent

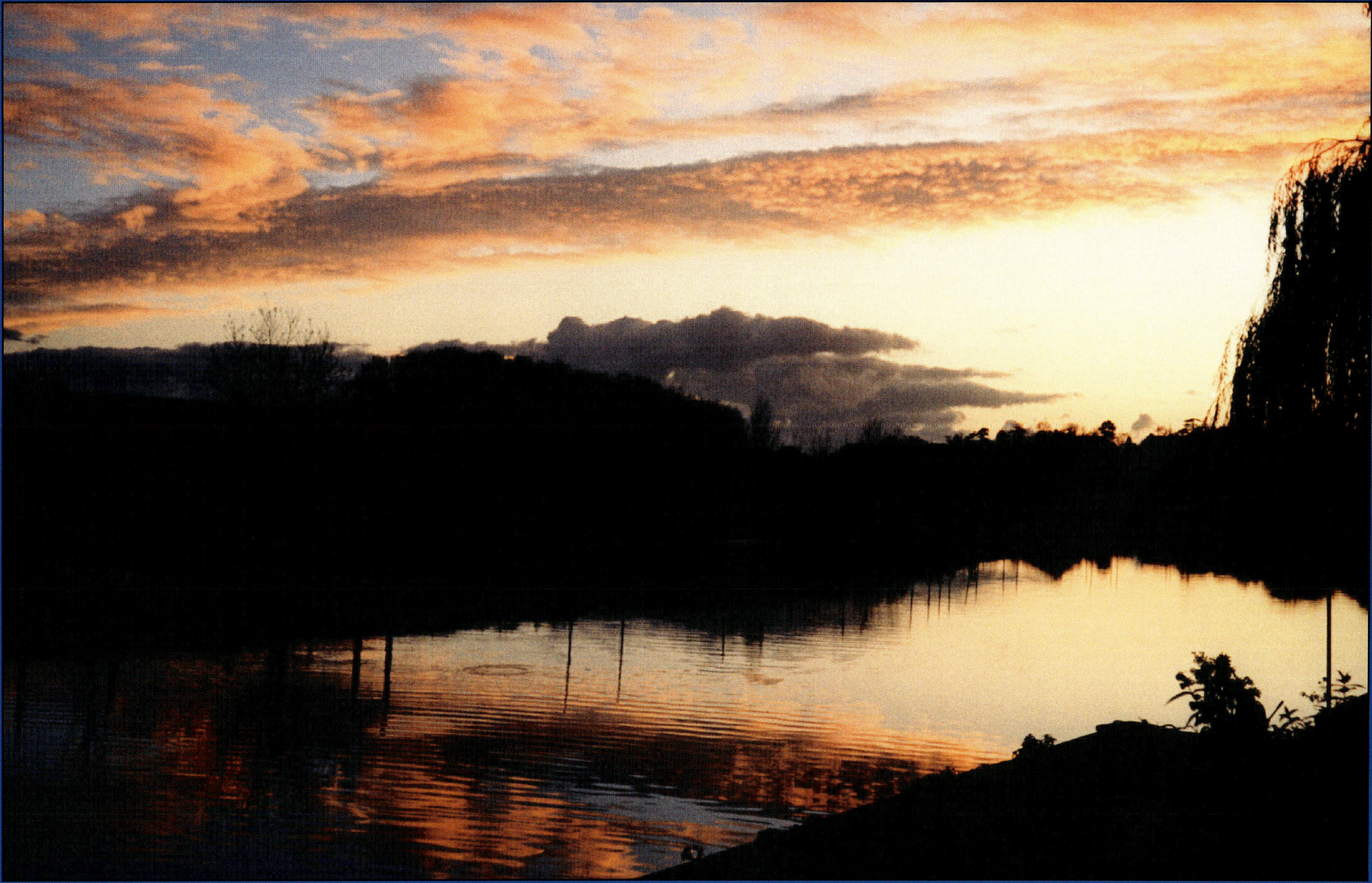

Photo by David Evans

images **of Kent**

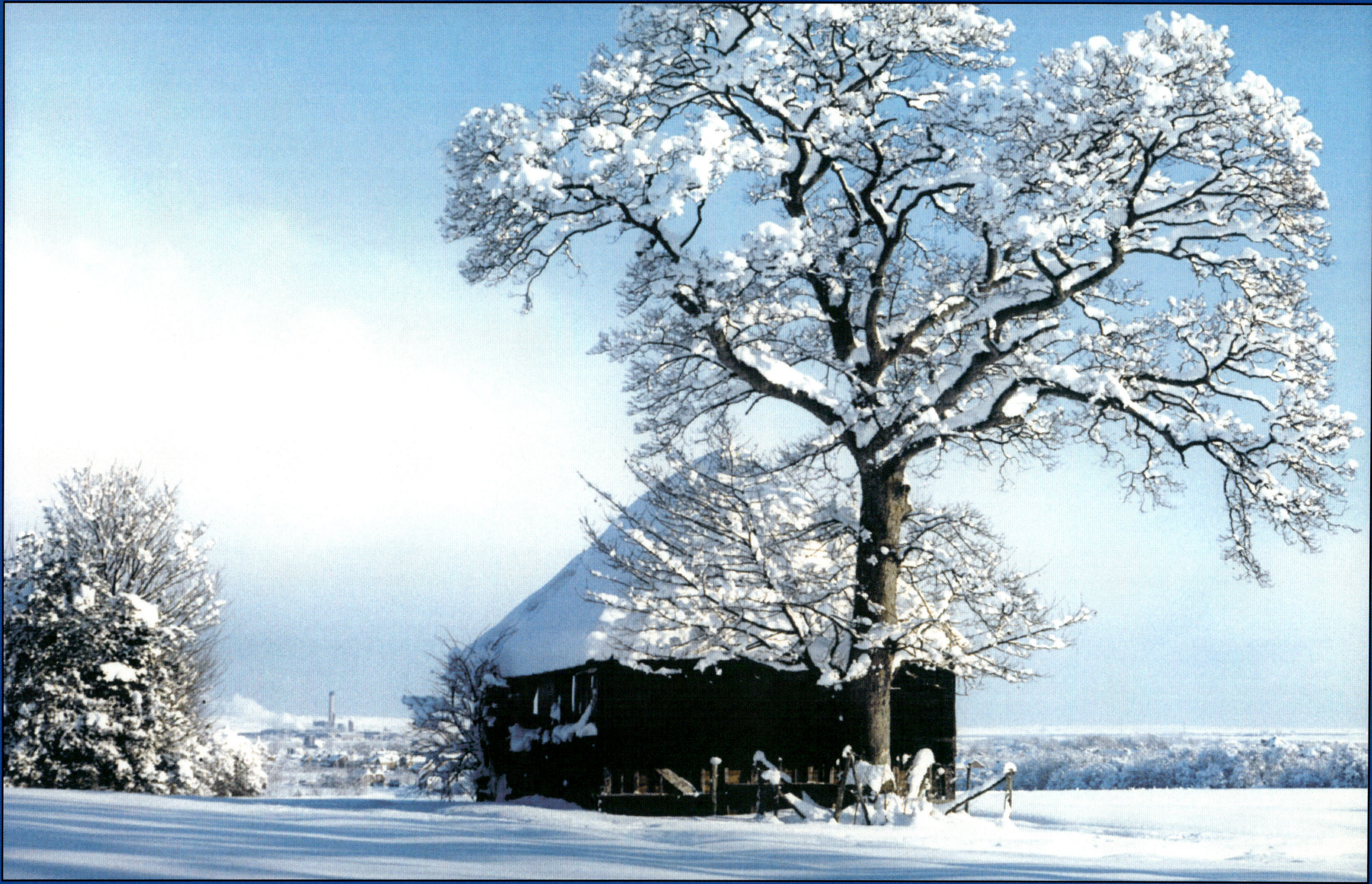

Photo by Arthur J Page FRPS

Photo by EP Ashdown

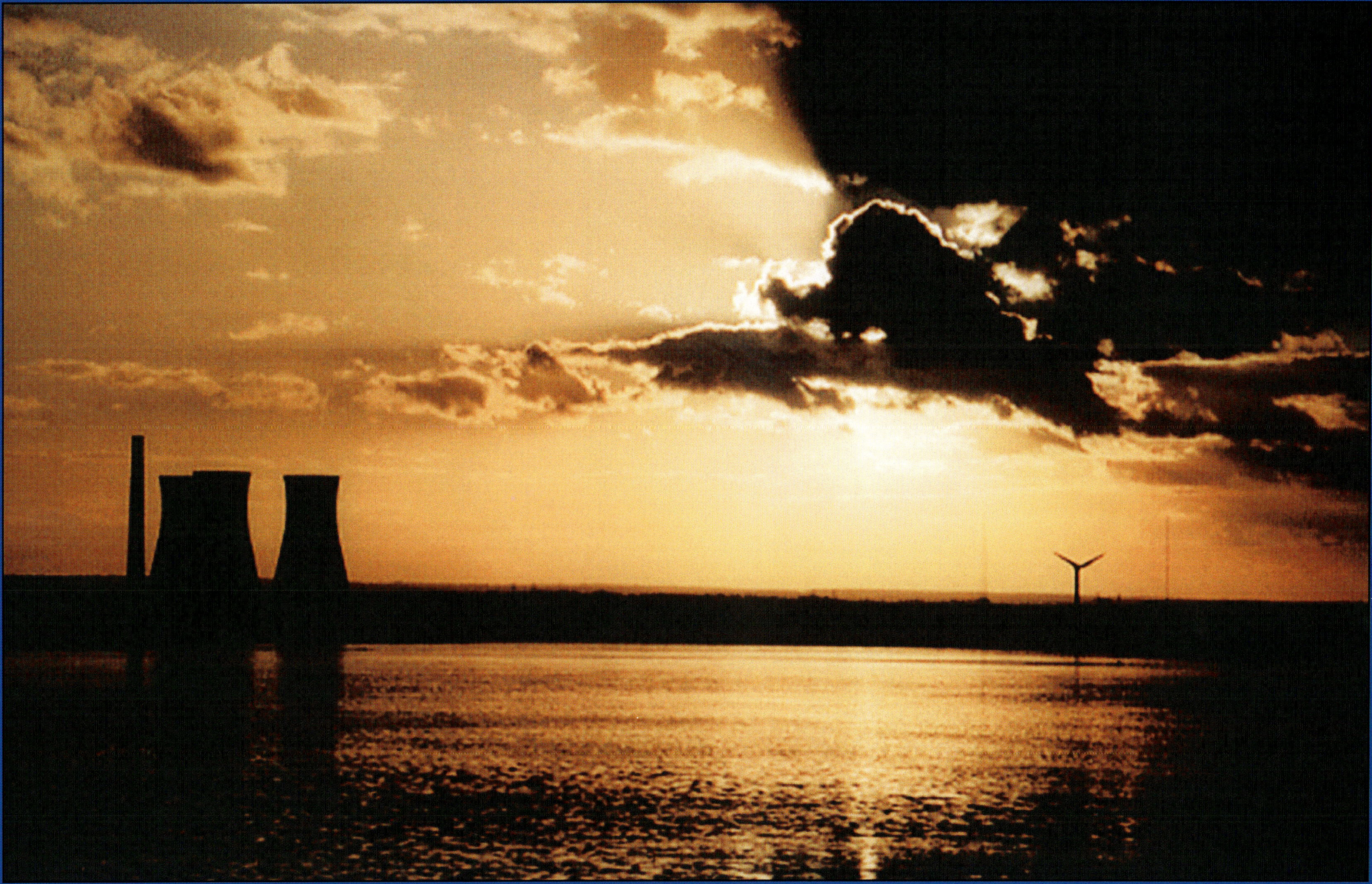

233 Richborough Towers

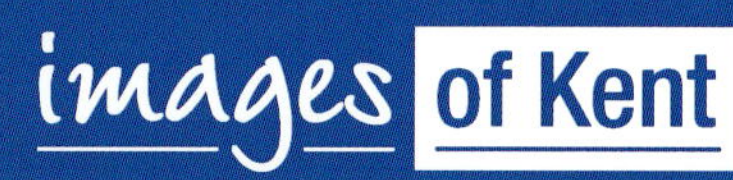

Photo by Martin Howard

Photo by David Bowie

Photo by Stephen Benzie

images of Kent

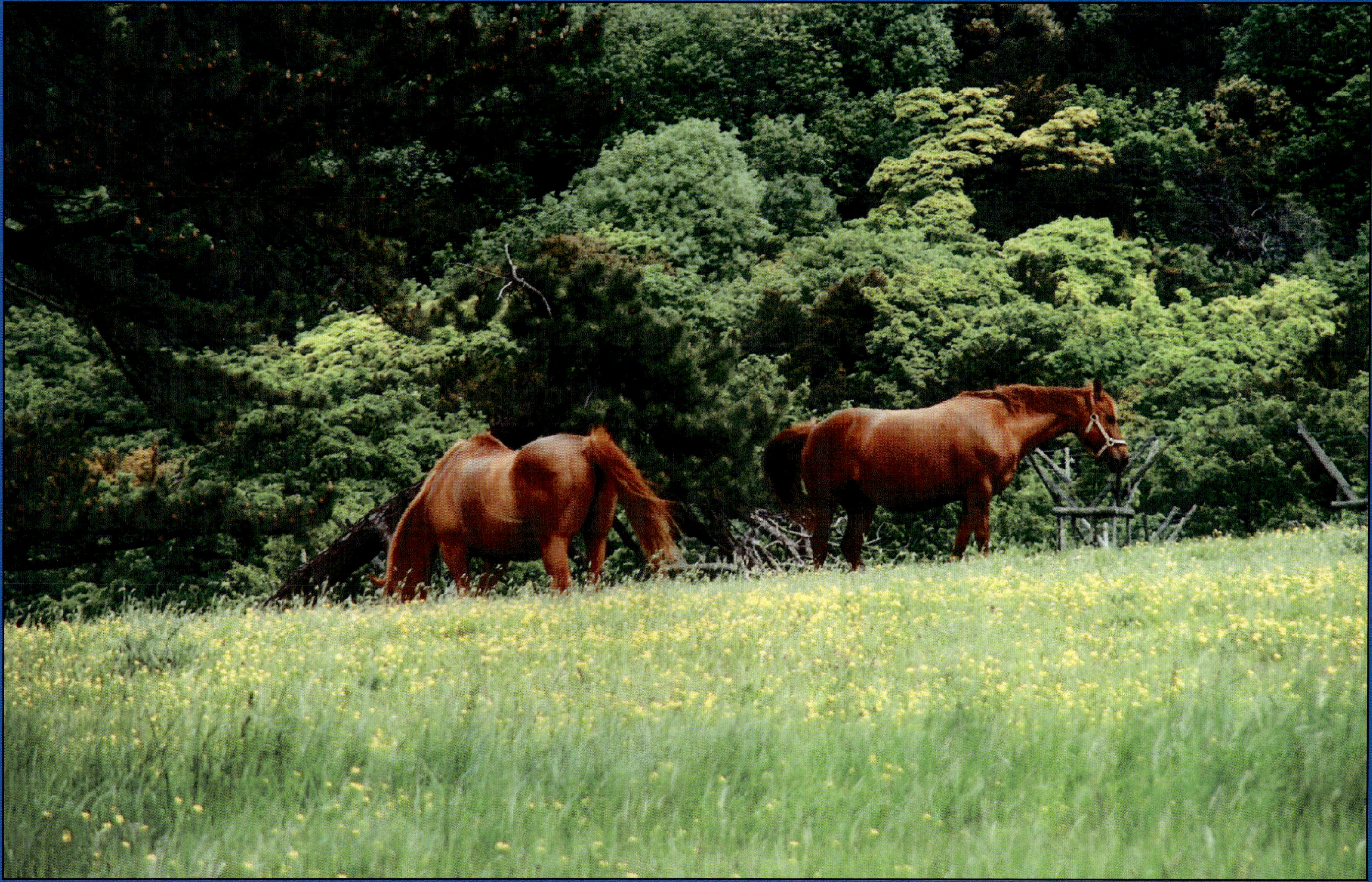

  The North Downs above Boxley Village, near Maidstone

Photo by Steve Lavin

INDEX